# SPEEDREADING:
# The How-to Book
# For Every Busy Manager,
# Executive, and Professional

# SPEEDREADING:
## The How-to Book
## For Every Busy Manager,
## Executive, and Professional

Diana Darley Fink

John T. Tate, Jr.

Michael D. Rose

John Wiley & Sons, Inc.
New York • Chichester • Brisbane • Toronto • Singapore

Publisher: Judy Wilson
Editors: Dianne Littwin and Karen Hess
Production Manager and Designer: Evelyn M. Fazio
Art: Mary M. Williams

**Library of Congress Cataloging in Publication Data**

Fink, Diana
 Speedreading, the how-to book for every busy
manager, executive, and professional.

 (Wiley self-teaching guides)
 Includes index.
 1. Rapid reading.  I. Tate., John,
II. Rose, Michael D.,  . III. Title.
IV. Series.
LB1050.54.F54   428.4'3   81-10373
ISBN 0-471-08407-7   AACR2
Printed in the United States of America
82  83  10  9  8  7  6  5  4  3  2

To all of our teachers who said to us, "Yes."

# Preface

Reading takes time. Time is a commodity that you, as a professional in the public or private sector, cannot afford to waste, any more than you can afford to mismanage any other investment. In order to fully capitalize on this major investment in your professional growth, you must read efficiently. That is why the words "speed reading" are somewhat misleading, unless you combine the elements of quantity *and* quality into your understanding of the term. To make the best use of your time means not only to read rapidly, but also to satisfy your needs for comprehension of the material. Thus, if you are to realize the full benefits of your reading time, you must learn to READ SMARTER, NOT JUST FASTER.

This book shows you how to read smarter from the first chapter as you assess your present skill level in concrete terms. Most people have vague misgivings about their present reading abilities, but have never defined them in measurable terms. In subsequent chapters, you learn why you read slowly by identifying your old, ineffective habits and replacing them with well-defined, effective, new habits. The first improvement is in your speed, as you learn how it is possible to read and understand more words per minute. You learn that your new speed skill is not magic, but rather a physical skill that requires method and practice. Once the foundation of the speed skill has been set, the comprehension improvement of the skill is built. After combining the quantity and the quality components of smart reading, the techniques for reading various types of technical or narrative information are developed, because the effective reader must apply the correct speed and comprehension techniques to meet the demands of each reading situation. Two complementary skills are presented to augment and expand the professional's reading repertoire: concentration and memory improvement. Finally, the methods to maintain the skills are listed, with exercises to reinforce them into becoming a life-long component of your work.

Although the reading selections used in the lessons for practice are presented with the professional person in mind, the course is easily translated to small seminar or college use. Practice in your own reading materials is encouraged, in order to tailor the skills to your particular needs.

Effective reading is a vehicle for enhancing your job knowledge and ability. The norm in today's world seems to be shortages of personnel who can demonstrate basic skills, coupled with increased reading requirements and less available time. In this atmosphere, the effective reader is more readily promotable. The ironic statement, "I don't have time to take a speed reading course, I have too much to read," typifies the trap which places many people behind an ever-growing pile of "must-read's" that are never read. By investing wisely in your skills of faster and smarter reading, you will join many professionals who have transformed their demanding reading requirements from predicaments into opportunities.

# Acknowledgments

Our thanks go to:

Joanna Cadwallader for her typing and her patience;

Patrick Dodd for his advice and his talent;

Mary Williams for her drawings;

Elaine Tannenbaum for designing the cover;

Carol Tate for her patience;

Jeff and Jon Fink for their time and feedback.

# Contents

## CHAPTER 6: Developing Your Memory

What Is Memory? Types of Memory. Short-Term Memory. Tips for a More Efficient Short-Term Memory System. Types of Remembering. Long-Term Memory: Review Is the Key. Four Stages of Review. Nature of the Review Session. Conclusions.

## CHAPTER 7: Putting It All Together

Summary and Final Testing. A Final Word.

# 1 ——————————————— Why Speed Reading?

*"I don't have time to take a speed reading class, I have too much to read."*

Are you frequently faced with a stack of papers, brochures and memos that demand reading, yet have no time to do it? Or have you needed to read a large, imposing book, but despaired of even picking it up, knowing you would never finish it? Even if you took time to read every word, some of it would be irrelevant and consequently a waste of your working time. So, you let the stack of "must reads" get higher and higher—you'll read it when the time is right. The right time never comes, however, so you finally throw the stack out, unread, and you feel guilty. This cycle repeats itself, but through the years, the stack gets larger and larger as your reading requirements for keeping abreast with the constant information flow in your field enlarges.

Professionals cannot safely assume that the state of the art in their particular profession has reached a standstill. True professionals must pay constant attention to new, developing information in the field, a pleasant or an unpleasant job, depending on the reader's skills in acquiring new information.

Are you spending more time at work reading? Is your reading material piling up? Do you read everything that crosses your desk in the same manner? Do you find yourself taking reading home with you? Check the following types of material that you read at work.

_____ policy manuals and update reports

_____ state and national government publications

_____ memos

_____ promotional literature

_____ progress and status reports

_____ environmental impact reports

_____ position papers

_____ proposals

Many professionals have an ever-increasing amount of printed information to digest each day. Some of the information is superfluous to the job and must be recognized as such and discarded. Other information is essential to the day-to-day operation of business or administrative procedure. Yet other information relates to current developments in a particular field. Such information is critical and must be absorbed and used professionally. Thus, the professional reading requirements are two-fold: (1) wading through the garbage and quickly discarding it and (2) absorbing the good, important material quickly, with good comprehension and retention.

Reflect for a minute on how much technical reading you do each day. How many hours do you spend reading material you *have* to read, not what you *want* to read?

_____ hours
What percent of the material do you comprehend?

_____ percent
How high is your level of concentration?

_____ low _____ medium _____ high

If you believe that these three areas hinder you from ever getting to the material you *want* to read, consider the cost of reading too slowly in another way.

More than one-third of a typical manager's day is spent reading and learning. For a person who earns $21,000 per year, $7,000 pays for reading/learning time. You could learn to read 50 words per minute faster; that is 3,000 more words per hour, or 10 more book pages per hour. Fifty words per minute is an average increase in reading speed of approximately 20 percent. Doubling your effective reading speed is even more attainable or reasonable. If executives could learn to read the same amount of material in half the time, each executive would have an extra hour and a half per day to do other things and the company would save $3,500. Take a moment to calculate the dollar cost of your own reading time at work.

The problem usually is that, if the professional had an entire day to spend reading and absorbing the proper information, no time would remain to use the information. You are not allotted adequate time to read and evaluate everything that crosses your desk. Thus, you may feel overwhelmed with words. You might also feel words are manipulating you. Words in your job, on television, in the newspaper, all try to manipulate in some respect. For once, wouldn't it be nice to have the power to manipulate those words rather than the opposite.

One reason words may seem so overwhelming is that you read too slowly. By doing this, all that is apparent and obvious to you is words. But words are meaningless except in relation to one another. They are the building blocks on which the ideas that relate to your professional work are constructed. If you had a tool with which to harness all those words, to have them work for you rather than them seeming to be your taskmaster, then you could manipulate the words. That is what this book is about: *empowering you as a professional to do a better job*. Reading faster will mean you can read more and learn more about your job, while simultaneously having time to do other things that demand your attention.

## EFFICIENCY AND EFFECTIVENESS

The art of reading involves many distinct, complex skills. Each can be addressed individually and developed through practice. But until all the skills are amalgamated, there is no reading. Thus, a combination of an efficient rate with an effective level of comprehension is desirable for those who want to become skilled readers. People who "read" a novel in 10 minutes but cannot tell you a simple plot are not considered good readers—they are ineffective. On the other hand, those who can tell everything about the novel but who took two months to read it aren't good readers either—they are inefficient. This book will help you become effective and efficient in reading. Learning and practicing a good method of speed reading allows you to combine a faster rate with good comprehension.

## SOME SKILLS NECESSARY FOR GOOD READING

Rate yourself according to how well you perform each of the following skills.

|  | Needs Improvement | Pretty Good | Excellent |
|---|---|---|---|
| 1. Ability to read and comprehend at higher speeds. |  |  |  |
| 2. Ability to use a flexible rate according to purpose and difficulty. |  |  |  |
| 3. Ability to grasp the main ideas or central thought of material. |  |  |  |
| 4. Ability to grasp and retain detail. |  |  |  |
| 5. Overall good retention. |  |  |  |
| 6. Ability to recognize organization of written material and to reorganize if necessary. |  |  |  |
| 7. Ability to read critically and evaluatively. |  |  |  |

Some of the preceding skills are directly addressed in this book; for example, instruction in and exercise on comprehension and speed flexibility. Other skills are indirect benefits of reading more rapidly. For example, evaluative reading requires much background and exposure to large amounts of material in order to make comparisons. You will cover more material with your new ability to move through the material faster and retain more.

Equal emphasis is placed on improving reading speed and improving comprehension. You will learn concepts of more skillful reading, learn techniques to implement the concepts, and then practice drills to ensure that you understand and can readily use the new techniques.

You are about to begin a course of study that makes demands on you in terms of time and energy. However, at the end of this book, *if* you have followed the directions and have practiced for the requisite hours, you will read at higher rates and understand more. You will have a systematic method to absorb technical material quickly and efficiently. You will also acquire better powers of concentration and memory, and you will simultaneously become better informed about the reading process. The material in this book is non-fiction because the skills presented are concerned with material you *must* read, rather than material you *want* to read.

## REQUIREMENTS FOR IMPROVING READING SKILLS

Reaping the rewards of faster reading involves seven requirements:

1. *Desire to improve.* A sincere desire is essential for any improvement.

2. *Believe it is possible* to improve. The worst thing you can ask of any instructor is, "Teach me the impossible." You must believe it is possible; you may not know how, but you must believe there is a way. You may have friends who have taken a course in speed reading or are naturally fast readers. If so, you have experienced first-hand the possibility of reading and comprehending at higher rates of speed.

3. *Follow all directions* carefully. The instruction has been pared to the vital elements of good speed reading. Any deviation or omission of instructions or lessons will seriously impair your ability to perform the skills described.

4. *Compete with yourself.* Try to improve with each exercise. Each person reading this book will begin at a different level. Therefore, compete only with yourself. Make each exercise another step towards improved reading.

5. *Develop a systematic approach* to reading. Starting with each chapter in this book, look for the organization of each chapter (the format is explained later) and make sure you understand what you are required to learn and do. Study and practice the skills systematically and consistently.

6. *Guard against tension.* In the speed exercises, some people get a little tense. Tension may negatively affect comprehension. Obviously, comprehension suffers if you are nervous while doing the exercises. Remember, it is possible to be mentally alert, yet physically relaxed.

7. *Practice.* Emphasis on diligent practicing appears throughout the book because the only way to trade in a lifetime of old reading habits is to understand and reinforce the new habits. Otherwise, you will easily slip back into your old ways of doing things, quite understandably, because old habits are comfortable and familiar. The only way to make the new habits comfortable and familiar is to reinforce them through practice.

The one prerequisite you need for this course is the ability to read at approximately an eighth grade level, the level of most daily newspapers. If you find yourself having a hard time pronouncing common words, if you can't follow the storyline of newspaper articles, if the vocabulary of most of the articles is not understandable, or if English is a new language for you, you may want to consider a reading clinic at your nearest adult school or college before you begin this book.

## TASKS/HOW TO USE THIS BOOK

Before reading each chapter, take a few minutes to look through the entire chapter. Note subheadings, diagrams, and questions. This preliminary overview enables you to better understand the information in the chapter.

Each chapter is one lesson. The chapters should be studied in order. Each chapter requires you to practice exercises in that chapter for about one week before moving to the next chapter. This rate of progression is especially important in Chapters 3, 4 and 6.

Progress through the book at your own pace. Take as long as you need to understand the theory portion of each chapter. The practical application portion (the exercises and readings), however, requires you to be concerned with how fast you read. You may notice that some chapters move faster than others. This is normal. Don't be concerned with an irregular pace through the different chapters because some chapters are more demanding than others.

The chapters present theory first and then exercises to put that theory into practice. The theory may describe some aspect of reading or the rationale behind a new skill. Periodically, there are short progress checks to assure that you grasp the main points. The main goal of the theory is to help you perform well on practice exercises. The practice exercises at the end of each chapter validate your new skills by self-testing and are designed to be used throughout that week's practice program.

The week-long practice exercises require you to use your own materials, making them valid experiences for a large cross-section of people. You can address your needs effectively if you get some of your "must" reading done while you improve your reading skills. The reading selections at the end of the chapters help you see your skills develop and let you acquire useful information while you practice.

## YOUR PROGRESS/RECORD KEEPING

The record of your progress on the chart in the back of the book (on page 193) aids in developing your skills. Records offer encouragement; they help to analyze progress by spotting weak areas, strong areas, and learning plateaus.

The test you take at the end of this chapter is designed to give you a point from which to measure your improvement in reading. The test is not meant to be particularly difficult, and should not be taken as anything but an indication of your current status. The end of chapter tests are specifically designed to measure the particular skills presented in that chapter. Those tests are also designed to show your growth in reading efficiency.

This book can be an aid wherever and whenever you can find the time to learn. The structure provides short periods of learning theory, and then the opportunity for distributed practice. This structure offers you flexibility in designing a course of study to meet the demands on your available time.

You may find some associates in your company who would like to take instruction with you, take the tests, and compare their progress with yours. Make sure the atmosphere is supportive rather than too competitive.

Many articles advocating more effective employee/employer relationships stress the necessity for everyone to use available time well. You get only 60 minutes per hour, no matter how far up the ladder you ascend. One method frequently recommended in such articles is to improve reading skills. Improvement may involve a decision not to read the material at all if it is not pertinent to your needs. You may decide to determine only the general idea of the material, or you may decide to give a particular selection your close attention for an in-depth reading and study. Whichever the case, to make the most of your work/study time, you must choose the correct procedure for reading and effectively apply it to everything that comes across your desk.

### TIPS FOR DOING WELL IN THIS COURSE

1. Be optimistic—maintain a positive mental attitude. Look for the positive in whatever you attempt with this book.

2. Keep an open mind—remember, you don't read fast enough right now, so you must do something differently. Accept the fact that many people read faster than you because they know something about reading that you don't, whether or not they can verbalize it. Don't prejudge something until you have given it a fair and honest try.

3. Don't over-intellectualize the course. People tend to over-intellectualize material when they are afraid to try something new. If you find yourself doing that as you progress, read Chapter 2's section again on changing habits, and try to relax and have fun with the book.

4. Try it. Consistently review what you have already learned by practicing. Make the new skills meaningful through consistent, personal application.

### ASSESSING YOUR CURRENT READING SKILLS

Few people know with any certainty how well or how fast they read. Most professionals we encounter express anywhere from a vague discomfort to outright despair about their reading skills, based solely on the stacks on their desks that never seem to shrink.

The following selection will give you a measure of your current reading speed and comprehension. It is *not* the final word on your present reading ability; that is impossible unless you could be personally tested. View this activity, instead as a starting point as you begin to acquire new and more effective reading skills.

Read the following selection as you normally read. Some people are tempted to push themselves to achieve higher speeds, but this is at the expense of comprehension. Others are tempted to memorize every word because they know a comprehension check follows the reading. Try to make this selection an accurate reflection of how fast you read and how well you understand.

Time yourself so you can compute how many words per minute you read. Look at a clock or watch with a sweep second hand and jot down the minute and seconds at which you begin to read. Read the selection and note the ending time. Answer the comprehension questions that follow the selection. Be brief. Check your answers in the back of the chapter.

---

**Reading Selection**

**Title:** *The Capacity to Generate Language Viability Destruction*
**Author:** Edwin Newman

    1. Read the article

        a. beginning time:_____

        b. ending time:_____

        Total number of minutes to read the article_____
                (b minus a equals total number of minutes)

    2. Answer questions and check your answers at the end of the chapter. Give yourself 20 percent for each correct answer.

    3. Compute words per minute. Divide the total number of words in the article (2,544) by the minutes you took to read it.

    4. Record speed and comprehension on the Course Progress Chart in the Appendix.

# The Capacity to Generate
# Language Viability Destruction

Edwin Newman

At one time Edwin Newman was best known as a television newsman. In recent years, however, his books on the decline of English have also made him one of the country's more prominent authorities on the use and misuse of language. The following excerpt is taken from his first best-selling book *Strictly Speaking*.

The business instict is by no means to be sneered at. I have had only one moneymaking idea in my life. It came to me like a flash (though not from Mr. Tash, the manager of a jewelry store in Washington, D.C., after the Second World War, and the inspiration of a radio commercial which began, "Now here's a flash from Mr. Tash—If you'll take a chance on romance, then I'll take a chance on you," meaning that he sold engagement and wedding rings on credit). It came to me like a flash one day when I was thinking about the growth of the population and the domination of American life by the automobile.

I fell to wondering, as any red-blooded American would, how some money might be made from that combination of factors, and I conceived the idea that because walking as a pleasure was becoming a lost art, a great deal of money might be made by settling up a pedestrians' sanctuary, a place where people could walk. I saw in my mind's eye the name *Walkorama*, or *Strollateria*, or something of the sort, and a place that would require little in the way of outlay or upkeep—just some space, grass, trees, and quiet. Obviously it would need a parking lot so that people could drive to it and park their cars before entering the walkorama to walk, and I intended to hold on to the parking concession for myself.

Nothing came of it. It was a typically footless newsman's dream, like the little weekly with which to get back to real people, dispense serene wisdom, and go broke, in Vermont.

I do not, therefore, sneer at the men and women of business. If they were not buying time on NBC, the world might or might not be a poorer place, but I would unquestionably be a poorer inhabitant of it.

However, the contributions of business to the health of the language have not been outstanding. Spelling has been assaulted by Duz, and E-Z Off, and Fantastik, and Kool and Arrid and Kleen, and the tiny containers of milk and cream catchily called the Pour Shun, and by products that make you briter, so that you will not be left hi and dri at a parti, but made welkom...

In many such monstrosities, the companies involved know what they are doing. In others they often do not, especially when it is a matter of grammar. New York remains the business capital of the United States, on a typical day there you may pick up the *New York Times,* or that paragon of eastern sophistication, the *New Yorker* magazine, and find a well-known Fifth Avenue jeweler telling the world that "The amount of prizes Gubelin has won are too numerous to be pure chance." I happen to know that this was a straw man Gubelin was knocking down because nobody had said it were pure chance. The sentiment in the circles I travel in was that the amount of prizes were fully deserved.

In the same advertisement Gubelin also gives us the following: "Sculpture II, an 18 carat white-gold ring with 24 diamond baguettes and two smoky quartzes, fancy cut, is a unique work of art to be worn on one finger, and without doubt rightly among the Gubelin creations that have taken the Diamonds-International Award." Turning the word rightly into a verb is no small achievement, but it should have been rightlies, so that the advertisement would read, "...and without doubt rightlies among the Gubelin creations that have taken the Diamonds-International Award."

Another possible verb is gubelin. "I have gubelined," he said, hanging his head, "and I no longer rightly among you, winners all of the Diamonds-International Award." He turned and walked falteringly toward the door.

"For a moment it seemed that the high priest, or Tiffany, was about to forgive him, but it was not to be. 'Go,' the Tiffany said, pointing to the outer darkness, 'go and gubelin no more.'" ...

Most business language is not so evocative. It is simply wrong. Gulf Oil used to speak of "one of the most unique roadways ever built," which of course helped Gulf to be ready for what it so long claimed to be ready for— "Whatever the work there is to be done." TWA has long had it Amarillio, not Amarillo, Texas; B. Altman in New York advertises sweaters that are "definitly for a young junior"; Bergdorf Goodman makes it known that "an outstanding selection of luxurious furs are now available at tremendous reductions"; Cartier believes that a memorandum pad, a stationery holder, and a pencil cup make a triumverate; the Great Lakes Mink Association wrote a letter to a New York store, the Tailored Woman, referring to its "clientel," and the Tailored Woman was happy to print it in an advertisement, though I do not say that this is what caused the Tailored Woman to close down; the chain of men's stores, Broadstreet's, capitalizing on the growing interest in food, tried to sell some of its wares by spreading the word that "Good taste is creme sengelese soup in a mock turtleneck shirt from Broadstreet's," but the number of people in New York familiar with, or curious about, sengelese cooking must have been small, and even the later announcement, "We shrunk the prices on our premium men's stretch hose," did not keep

Broadstreet's from disappearing from the New York scene. Hunting World, a New York shop, sells Ella Phant, "pride and joy of the Phant family," and say, "She's only 9″ tall, and every little people you know will love her and you will too." Perhaps that depends on the kind of little people you know. Every little people that some of us know probably would be more interested in the Selig Imperial Oval Sofa, advertised by the Selig Manufacturing Company of Leominster, Massachusetts, which noted that "an orgy of 18 pillows, all shapes and colors, make a self-contained environment." An orgy do a lot of other things also.

Business language takes many forms. Camaraderie: "Us Tareyton smokers would rather fight than switch." Pomposity: When Morgan Guaranty Trust announced that negotiable securities worth $13,000,000 were missing from its vaults, it said, "A thorough preliminary search for the securities has been made, and a further search is now being made." All it needed to say was, "We're looking for them" —if indeed it couldn't expect its distinguished clients to take for granted that it was looking.

Pseudo science: "You are about to try the most technologically advanced shaving edge you can buy. Wilkinson Sword, with a world-wide reputation for innovation, brings you still another advance in razor blade technology, the first third-generation stainless steel blade. First, a microscopically thin layer of pure chromium is applied to the finely ground and stropped edge. Then, another layer of a specially developed chromium compound is applied. This special layer of chromium compound adds extra qualities of hardness, durability and corrosion resistance. Finally, a thin polymer film is coated onto the edge. This coating allows the blade to glide smoothly and comfortably over your face." Shaving seems an inadequate employment for so distinguished a product of razor blade technology, but even technology cannot hold back the dawn, and the razor is going the way of the reaper and the cotton gin. We are now invited to use the Trac-2 shaving system, which apparently is to the razor as the weapons system is to the bow and arrow. Much more of this might make you want to use the first third-generation stainless steel blades, or even the Trac-2, to slit your throat.

Stainless steel I may not be, but I was the first third-generation American in my family, on either trac, to hear life jackets carried on airliners referred to as articles of comfort. It was on a flight from London to New York in 1966, and the stewardess began her little lecture by saying, "Because of our interest in your comfort, we will now demonstrate your life jackets." It was a wonderful notion, classifying the gadget to be used after a plane has gone down in the North Atlantic as part of the comfort of flying. Euphemistic business language can go no further. Only calling used cars preowned has, in my experience, equaled it....

When business turns its attention from customers to shareholders, the change in tone is drastic. Customers must be tempted and/or bullied; shareholders must be impressed and intimidated, wherefore the annual corporate reports. Something like six or seven thousand of these are issued every year, but the language is so nearly uniform that they may all be written by a single team, as paperback pornographic novels are written wholesale in porno novel factories. (I was about to say, sweatshops, but I assume that for reasons already made clear, the sweatshop either is no more or exists only where perverseness bordering on un-Americanism lingers on.)

In the pornos, what counts is the detailed description of sexual enterprise. In corporate reports it is growth, which at the very least should be significant, and with any luck at all will be substantial. The ultimate for growth is to be dynamic. Whether it is, and whether it occurs at all, depends largely on growth opportunities; if they occur often enough, a consistent growth pattern may be achieved, brought about, perhaps, by an upward impetus that makes things move not merely fast but at an accelerated rate.

No company can grow, of course, without having a growth potential. To realize that potential, the company must have capabilities: overall capabilities, systems capabilities, flexible capabilities, possibly nuclear services capabilities, generating capabilities, environmental control capabilities, predictability capabilities. If all of these are what they should be, and the company's vitality, viability, and critical reliability are what *they* should be, the growth potential will be realized, and profitability should result.

There are, however, other factors that must mesh. Outlooks, solutions, and systems must be sophisticated, or, if possible, highly sophisticated or optimal. Innovative products are requisite; they, in turn, are the consequence of innovative leadership that keeps its eye firmly on target areas, on inputs and outputs, on components and segments and configurations. Innovative leadership does this because capabilities are interrelated so that requirements, unwatched, may burgeon. For example, after a corporation has identified the objective of getting a new facility into start-up, environmental-impact reporting requirements must be met so that the facility can go on-stream within the envisaged time-span.

Even this tells only the bare bones of the story. Multiple markets and multi-target areas may well be penetrated, but not without impact studies, market strategies, cost economies, product development and product packaging, and consumer acceptance. Product packaging sounds simple enough, but it may call for in-hour box-making capability. Box-making in turn is a process; that calls for process equipment capability; and *that* calls for process development personnel.

If all this is to be done, management teams must be sound and prudent and characterized by vision, enterprise, and flexibility. In a surprising number of companies, the corporate reports assure us, management teams are.

Business puts enormous pressure on language as most of us have known it. Under this pressure, triple and quadruple phrases come into being—high retention characteristics, process knowledge rate development, anti-dilutive common stock equivalents. Under this pressure also, adjectives become adverbs; nouns become adjectives; prepositions disappear; compounds abound.

In its report on 1972, American Buildings Company told its shareholders that its new products included "improved long-span and architectural panel configurations which enhance appearance and improve weatherability." Despite the travail concealed behind those simple words, the achievement must have been noteworthy on the cutting edge of the construction industry.

A statement by the Allegheny Power System was, on the other hand, hardly worth making: "In the last analysis the former, or front-end process seems the more desirable because the latter, or back-end, process is likely to create its own environmental problems." This is an old story, for the front-end process often does not know what the back-end process is doing.

In its annual report for 1972, Continental Hair Products drove home two lessons. One was that "Depreciation and amortization of property, plant and equipment are provided on the straight-line and double declining balance methods at various rates calculated to extinguish the book values of the respective assets over their estimated useful lives."

Among Continental's shareholders, one suspects, sentimentalists still quixotically opposed to the extinguishing of book values may have forborne to cheer. But not the others, and they must have been roused to still greater enthusiasm by the outburst of corporate ecstasy which was the second point: "Continental has exercised a dynamic posture by first establishing a professional marketing program and utilizing that base to penetrate multi-markets."

For myself, looking at this array of horrors, I forbear to cheer. People are forever quoting Benjamin Franklin, coming out of the Constitutional Convention in 1787, being asked what kind of government the Convention was giving the country, and replying, "A republic—if you can keep it." We were also given a language, and there is a competition in throwing it away. Business is in the competition and doing nicely.

## Newman Comprehension Questions

1. What was Mr. Newman's money-making idea?


2. Companies are, according to Newman, destroying:

_____ a. competition

_____ b. grammar

_____ c. the shaving industry

_____ d. themselves.

3. The primary development of his argument uses:

_____ a. personal experience

_____ b. example

_____ c. logic

_____ d. exposition.

4. What change in attitude does business have when it turns its attention from customers to shareholders?


5. What is Newman's attitude about the future of our language?

## CONCLUSION

The next chapter, Chapter 2, introduces the general nature of habits, the process involved in changing reading habits, and the various alternatives available. If you are to change some aspect of your behavior (reading), then you must know exactly what you do now (old habits) and what options are available to you for change (new reading habits).

Chapter 3 concentrates on improving your speed, presenting the new physical skill needed to read more efficiently. To increase reading efficiency, you must first increase your speed and then improve the quality of your comprehension. Comprehension is addressed fully in Chapters 4, 5, and 6.

Because reading is not a collection of isolated functions, but rather an integrated process, Chapter 7 summarizes all the information in the book. Each aspect of reading improvement can be presented and explained separately, but then the overall process must be viewed and understood. Chapter 7 also provides a final test as a means of gauging your improvement from your first test.

### Your Goals

Set some course goals before you continue. These will be open for amendment as you move through the book. Most people don't have any idea of what their reading goals should be. Your expectations will influence your final result. If you plan to follow all directions, move through the material conscientiously and practice enough, you can expect to read three to five times faster, with equal or better comprehension. Take a minute and fill in your course goal:

I expect to be reading _____words per minute with equal or better comprehension. My expectations will be realized *if* I follow all directions and practice the requisite number of hours. I will allow myself to amend this goal as I see fit during the program of instruction if I believe it is necessary.

Now that you have some idea of how the book is organized, realize the factors that will help you on your way to faster reading, and know your present skill level, you are ready to begin. The speed increase and comprehension improvement you are about to learn will have a direct and exciting impact on your reading experience at work. If you could increase 50 words per minute while keeping comprehension high, that adds up to 3,000 more words per hour. Three thousand more words an hour means ten more pages of an average text, or perhaps ten more brochures and reports in an hour. Make a commitment to realize that type of improvement in your work life by learning in Chapter 2 what you can do to read faster and smarter.

**Answers: Newman article**

1. *A walkorama,* a pedestrian's sanctuary.
2. b.
3. b.
4. To impress and intimidate.
5. Business is destroying language.

# 2 ═══════════════════════ The Reading Process: Good and Bad Habits

*Spanish proverb: Habits are at first cobwebs, then cables.*

### IMPROVE YOUR READING SKILLS TO MAKE THE MOST OF YOUR TIME

It is up to you to select the correct process for reading, and then use it with everything that you read on the job, in order to be more efficient. The following are five steps that will help you improve your reading.

### FIVE CRITICAL STEPS TO IMPROVE READING

To improve your reading, you must take five steps:

1. Establish a need to read faster.
2. Understand the reading process.
3. Understand why you read slowly.
4. Learn new, efficient reading habits.
5. Practice the new skills.

The first step is to establish a need to read faster. Without this need, you would not have selected this book. Many people have told us they feel overwhelmed with the daily reading loads their preofessions require and wish they could keep abreast of them.

After identifying the need, the second step is to understand the reading process, which is one purpose of this chapter. Associated with identifying the reading process is understanding the nature of the changes you will make to replace the bad habits that slow you down when you read. To change these long held habits, you must understand the general nature of habits, to be discussed in detail in this chapter.

The third step is to identify specific problems associated with the reading process, especially those that keep you reading slowly now.

The fourth step is to introduce the new habits to replace the old, inefficient ones.

The fifth and final step in improving your reading efficiency is to apply the theoretical information presented in this chapter through practice and drill.

## THE READING PROCESS—HOW?

Reading involves both physical and mental elements. Because the two aspects are not totally discrete, it is difficult to describe where the physical ends and the mental begins.

The main factors in accelerating reading have to do with the way your mind works rather than with the way your eyes move over the lines of print. You can, however, help yourself become more efficient by knowing something of what your eyes do when you read.

The primary physical aspect of reading is moving your eyes. The movements consist of three distinct activities: fixations, saccades, and return sweeps. *Fixations* occur when your eyes are stopped; the only opportunity you have to read. The movements between fixations are called *saccades*. If you have ever watched anyone else read, you have probably noticed the saccades. They are not smooth movements, but rather jerky and almost erratic. When your eyes reach the end of the line, they perform the third motion, the *return sweep.* Cumulatively, your eyes perform these three actions when you read.

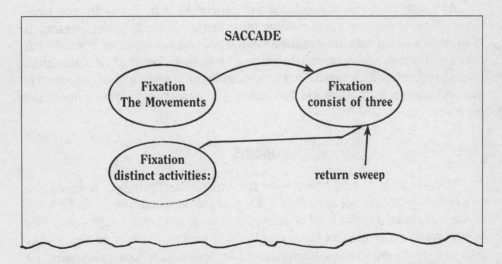

Reading experts disagree as to exactly what happens in the brain when you read. Varying theories exist as to the interface between language and the brain; that is, how the brain processes the information and how that information is then related to understanding. An in-depth discussion of brain function is beyond our scope here. Just remember that reading occurs in the brain, with the aid of your eyes.

Your eyes are an extension of your brain, functioning as sensory receptors or conduits from your external environment to your brain. Your brain uses these sensory receptors to collect information, written or otherwise.

Some understanding of how the brain functions in reading is useful in understanding the nature of reading. First, reading should be an active process, not a passive information dump. Second, the brain is capable of a tremendous level of activity, but when you read as you do now, you seldom tax your mental capacity. The methods and techniques presented in these lessons will teach you to actively approach reading and use more of your mental capacities.

Reading is analogous to computer work in that the print seen on a page is fed into your "computer" (the brain) and then decoded. Although this decoding process is not completely understood by the experts, agreement exists as to one essential aspect of decoding; that is, the reader must relate currently perceived information to previously stored information. When the new information is associated with information that was previously stored, it is "understood."

The term *reading* in this book is synonymous with understanding. When you are told to read in an exercise, or the word "comprehension" is used, you must try to understand the material to the best of your ability. You are the only real judge of the adequacy of your comprehension. That is why the term comprehension evades precise definition. When you are asked to read for understanding, do so given your present reading status.

Although portions of this book are concerned with the skills and techniques of rapid reading, speed reading must include accurate understanding. It is meaningless to talk of someone having a "reading speed of x words per minute," because speed cannot function in isolation. You read to understand. Consequently, "reading speeds" are only meaningful if you consider your level of comprehension, the nature and complexity of the material, and your needs and purposes.

## HABITS

Many of your reading habits were not formally taught to you. It would also be safe to say that no one actually sat down and showed you how to read a book, much less read it rapidly. That is primarily because not many people know how to read a book correctly, let alone rapidly. Your reading habits were acquired by trial and error, experiential learning, and by accident. It took many years for these habits to be incorporated into your learning system and you cling to them tenaciously. Your reading routine has become a battery of habits that you now perform unconsciously.

Webster defines a habit as, "an acquired mode of behavior that has become nearly completely involuntary." A habit could also be defined as a pattern of reptitious activity that lends stability to an unstable world. Some habits are positive, some potentially negative. Others simply cause us to be inefficient; for example, a typist looking at the keys. The inefficient habits must be replaced.

The most effective way to discard inefficient habits is to replace them with efficient ones. The emphasis is on replacing rather than discarding. When you discard a habit, some new behavior inevitably takes its place. You want to insure that the replacement behavior is beneficial to you, rather than leaving the replacement to chance.

As you progress through this book, you will replace old habits with new, more efficient habits. Chapter 3 will begin to threaten the old reading habits with new techniques. Remember that the old habits have been lodged in your reading behavior for a long time, so you must make a diligent, conscientious effort to replace them. The eminent social behaviorist, Max Weber, describes this replacement process as "freezing, unfreezing, and refreezing." That is, you were frozen into your old habits. This book will help you unfreeze out of them by teaching you to perform new reading techniques. Finally, you will refreeze into more efficient and effective reading habits.

Anxiety is a very typical reaction to unfreezing old habits. At some point in the instruction, you will probably experience some difficulty in reading either the old way or the new way. When you find yourself at the mid-way point, remember that you are discarding old habits and acquiring new ones. Don't give up hope! Anxiety should not be discouraging. If you are following the instructions, you are well on the way to a more secure and comfortable freeze into newer, faster, and more efficient reading habits. Although it can be an uncomfortable time, if you are sincere about changing something in your life that is not giving you enough satisfaction or time to do other things, you must be prepared to invest some time and effort. It *will* be worth it.

## GOOD READERS—WHAT DO THEY DO?

For many years observers have known that efficient readers have cultivated certain habits that allow them to read faster. These skills were either taught to them, were informally acquired through self-study, or sometimes were accidentally acquired. In any case, those good habits have been observed and analyzed.

Efficient readers read material at approximately 3-5 times the rate of the average reader. Efficient readers have smooth and rhythmic eye movements as they progress through the material, with few *regressions*—or rereading of the material. Their eyes are always in the intended place, rather than wandering over the page. They also have a wide span of focus on the words. They have reduced their level of *subvocalization*—saying words to themselves—to a minimum. Good readers also have a flexible, purposeful, systematic approach to many different types of material, as well as good concentration and memory. If you recognize in your own reading experiences the absence of any or all of the preceding habits, then you have taken a big step toward identifying why you read slowly.

## WHY YOU READ SLOWLY AND
## WHAT YOU CAN DO ABOUT IT

### Read Everything at the Same Speed

One inefficient reading habit is reading everything at approximately the same speed. If you read a journal article, a technical manual or anything of moderate difficulty, you read without much fluctuation in speed. This is not beneficial because certain materials are harder to comprehend. You should tailor your speed to the level of difficulty. The demands may also be higher if the vocabulary is new or you have limited background in the subject. Additionally, the material may be poorly arranged or poorly written. Any of these problems can cause a change in your reading speed. Until now, however, you have had no systematic method of changing your speed without sacrificing comprehension or wasting time by going too slowly.

A primary difference you will notice, as you become a more efficient reader, is that instead of reading at one speed, you will change both speed and technique according to the difficulty of the material and your reading purpose. As you expand your repertoire of speed and technique, you will have many more options for approaching reading material. Systematically applying the techniques will save a great deal of the time and effort you now waste when you read.

Do you tend to read everything at approximately the same speed?

_____yes  _____no  _____not sure

Along with the inefficient technique of reading everything at approximately the same speed, slow readers also exhibit some or all of the following characteristics.

### Inefficient Eye Motions

Some movements your eyes make when reading tend to slow your speed. The three major, inefficient activities are unnecessary regressions, unrhythmic eye motions, and faulty return sweeps.

### Unnecessary Regressions

Regression means to go back and reread material already read. If you are like the average reader, you will regress on 10 percent of the words you read. Many of the regressions are habitual, unnecessary, and unconscious. Purposeful, conscious regressions are not of concern because they are sometimes essential to comprehension. The majority of your regressions, however, are not purposeful and serve only to slow you down.

Do you feel that your eyes regress when you read?

\_\_\_\_\_yes  \_\_\_\_\_no  \_\_\_\_\_not sure

### Unrhythmic Motions

Unrhythmic eye motions are motions interrupting the smooth progression of fixations-saccades-return sweeps. Unrhythmic activities disturb the information flow to your brain and lower your concentration level. For example, if you try to read when you are tired, your eyes will tend to jump around the page. Even when you are well rested, the unaided eye tends to wander at the slightest provocation. Your eyes need assistance to eliminate these inefficient activities.

Do your eyes sometimes jump around on the page, especially when you are tired?

\_\_\_\_\_yes  \_\_\_\_\_no  \_\_\_\_\_not sure

### Faulty Return Sweeps

During the return sweep from one line to the next, the temptation arises for your eyes to wander rather than quickly return to the first word of the next line. This wastes time and effort. In fact, as much as 20 percent of the time wasted during reading results from faulty return sweeps. Your eyes need help to eliminate these inefficient activities.

Do you have faulty return sweeps?

\_\_\_\_\_yes  \_\_\_\_\_no  \_\_\_\_\_not sure

## Small Area of Fixation

Your eyes perceive about four words each time they fixate. The small number of words that you see results from the way you were taught to read: word by word. It is a reasonable way to learn to read, but you are using today essentially the same techniques as when you first learned to read. Reading that way, you do not fixate on enough words to increase your speed significantly. You must learn to see more words with each fixation.

Consider how much information your eyes take in when you are not reading. For instance, if you look at any object of book size held at arms' length, you see the entire object and a great deal of whatever surrounds it. You can transfer your ability to comprehend a larger field of information from your daily life to the reading process. The number of words you see in each fixation, your span of focus, can and must be increased before you can be a more efficient reader.

A quick exercise can demonstrate your learned span of focus in reading. Find a word in the middle of this page and stare at it. Without moving your eyes from that word, notice the area that surrounds your "word." You will notice the area is round, so you see words to the right and left, above and below your word. How many words in any direction can you see clearly? How many words in any direction are even discernable as English before they are perceived as just fuzzy designs on the page? Usually, an average field of focus has 4-6 words.

Now turn the book upside-down so you are looking at the page of print upside-down, then find another "word" and repeat the exercise. Notice that your eyes take in a much larger area, even though you can't read the word. Many more black scratches on the page are discernible. This is because your eyes don't recognize the scratches in the second exercise as words, thus relaxing their field of focus and allowing you to view the print as you would any other object in your visual field. This exercise illustrates that the number of words you can see per fixation is a learned habit. You can replace this inefficient habit with the more efficient one of increasing your span of focus to include more words.

After performing the exercise, do you feel you have a limited area of fixation?

_____yes   _____no   _____not sure

## Subvocalization

Subvocalization is saying the words to yourself as you read them. It is sometimes referred to as auditory reassurance.

Everyone subvocalizes when reading, some to a greater extent than others. If you are not sure whether you subvocalize or what it is like to subvocalize, go back to the paragraph on the small area of fixation and begin reading it aloud. Somewhere in the middle of the paragraph, stop saying the words aloud and read to yourself. You'll notice a "voice" in your head saying the words silently as you read. That "voice" is subvocalization.

Just like some of your other reading habits, you picked this one up long ago, when you were taught to read. You and your teacher needed assurance that you were learning the relationship between the letters and the sounds they represented. First, you saw the word, said it aloud, heard yourself say it, and then you were presumed to have understood it. Problems arise, however, when you attempt to apply elementary school reading methods and habits to your professional reading requirements. In 1966, Hardyck, Petrinovich and Ellsworth in their article in *Psycholinguistics and Reading* by Frank Smith, detailed an in-depth study of subvocalization, concluding the following:

> "There is a logical flaw in arguments based on the proposition that anything we do habitually or in times of stress must therefore be necessary and efficacious. Such an argument is, of course, simply a description of superstition. The fact that we tend to subvocalize only when our reading slows down ... suggests nothing more than a regression to classroom-induced behavior. Subvocalization is often regarded as a handicap to efficient reading and can be suppressed without the slightest detriment to comprehension."

As the three reading researchers concluded, subvocalization is not necessary for the efficient reader. First, efficient readers do not need to say all the words to themselves to understand their meaning because subvocalization is not a necessary component for comprehension. For your brain to allow your voice box to "say" a word, you must have first correctly perceived it. Secondly, subvocalization is inefficient; it slows your reading speed because you can subvocalize only a limited number of words per minute. Most people read at about 250 words per minute and speak at a far slower rate. If you could learn to speak faster, say 600–900 wpm, then you wouldn't need to change your old habit of subvocalization. (John Kennedy, clocked at the rate of 327 wpm, was considered the fastest speaker in public life according to the *Guiness Book of World Records.)*

If you read faster than 250 wpm as measured by the test in Chapter 1, you have already begun to drop some subvocalization. In fact, a mature reader (defined here as a person beyond the 8th grade level in reading ability) doesn't say every word on the page. A mature reader has stopped "saying" the "a's" and "the's," for example. If you read over 300 wpm on the initial test, you have begun to drop even more subvocalization. The reason you have done this is that you were bored. You also probably came to the conclusion, at least subconsciously, that you didn't have to say all the words to understand them.

Are you aware that you subvocalize?

_____yes _____no _____not sure

To *reduce* your subvocalization habits (even efficient readers never totally eliminate subvocalization), first understand that subvocalization is not necessary for comprehension. Next, make yourself read faster than you could possibly subvocalize. Remember, as you reduce subvocalization, you are purposely losing the reassurance that saying the words to yourself brings. Find some other forms of reassurance, and remember the general nature of reading habits needed to achieve the necessary confidence to overcome this problem. The following chapters will give various types of reassurance that you did, indeed, register all the words. The exercises have been designed to make you read faster than you could if you were subvocalizing all the words. You need supply only the effort and the belief that you can do it.

**Concentration**

Have you ever found yourself staring at the bottom of a page asking yourself, "How did I get here?" If so, then you understand what it is like to have poor concentration. Concentration is the ability to keep your attention directed wherever you want it. The external and internal distractions that make for poor concentration can be subtle killers of comprehension and motivation. The external distractions are discussed in Chapter 5, which is devoted specifically to concentration improvement. One major internal distraction, reading too slowly, is discussed in greater detail in Chapter 4.

Consider the potential capacity of your brain. It is capable of processing thousands of bits of information per minute. Consider next your old reading habits of, perhaps, 250 wpm. One major reason your mind wanders while you read (with the resulting poor concentration) is that your brain is "bored." Your brain looks for other work to do when you fail to give it enough. It is thinking about last week's fiscal report, next week's staff meeting, what you are planning this weekend ... anything but the printed material in front of you. When you learn to read faster, you will have better concentration right away.

Do you have poor concentration when you read? Do you think about other things when you read?

_____yes _____no _____not sure

**Memory**

After the reading process is completed, you need to remember the material; this is a separate and distinct process from comprehension. It is possible to have excellent comprehension of the material (remember, comprehension means understanding the text while reading it) and poor recall of the material a short time later.

One reason most people have problems remembering what they have read is that they read too slowly. Slow reading fragments the material. Because you read so slowly, you can't get an adequate perspective of the material. What slow readers usually remember after reading is an assortment of facts and details whose interrelationships are not readily apparent. Because these facts and details usually have no obvious relationship to one another, they are forgotten unless a great deal of time and effort is spent trying to memorize and reconstruct them for later use. It does not have to be that difficult.

Do you have trouble remembering what you have read?

_____yes _____no _____not sure

_____I forgot the question

Reading faster with a systematic method and well-defined purpose allows you to read for concepts and ideas. Most of us can remember a finite number of items with any success, usually around seven at a time. However, the number of concepts or ideas that we can remember has no limit. This is not to say you will disregard the facts, details, and supportive data. What it does mean is that soon you will avoid tedious rote memorization of those details. Instead you will make the ideas and concepts work for you, to help you remember the supportive data with far greater ease, reliability, and for a longer time. You will begin working on memory improvement in the following chapter and in Chapter 6, which is exclusively devoted to memory improvement.

List, in order of importance, the habits that are slowing you down when you read.

## SUMMARY

The way to read faster is to acquire a new set of skills and habits. Some efficient readers acquire these by trial and error over the years and, if asked how they read, would probably find it difficult to explain exactly which technique they use.

Trial and error is not a very sound basis for refining such a vital skill as reading. How can you improve your reading habits? To paraphrase the five steps at the beginning of this chapter, the most important factor is motivation. The stronger the motivation, the more quickly the skills are learned. The second most important factor is knowledge or a systematic method of implementing the new skills. Knowledge is essential, because motivation without knowledge and guidance leads to frustration. Because you have selected this book, you already have a certain amount of motivation. Now that you have read this chapter, you have a general knowledge of the skills necessary for efficient reading. But this knowledge will not help you much unless you incorporate it into your everyday reading requirements through patient and diligent application. Practice, then, is the third important factor necessary for you to become a successful speed reader.

At times, during your progress through the lessons, you will need to return to this chapter and reread certain sections. Issues and problems presented in this chapter are predictive. Sometimes you need the reassurance of satisfactory progress or the knowledge that the problems you encounter are typical of others' progress through the course. Feel free to return and reread the material on changing old habits. These discussions may take on more meaning as you actually begin building the skills.

Quickly review the chapter by noting the terms presented, then quiz yourself on their definitions.

To master any body of information, you must master its special vocabulary. To gain a working knowledge of the information, you must know the terms used in this chapter. Some were probably already familiar to you, but be sure that your definitions and ours coincide. Write a brief definition of each term. Check your answers with those provided at the end of the chapter.

**Vocabulary of Reading Quiz**

1. Fixation

2. Comprehension

3. Recall

4. Read

5. Subvocalization

6. Regression

7. Return sweep

8. Habit

9. Concentration

10. Auditory reassurance

11. Field of focus

12. Unfreezing

**Progress Check 1**

1. List three ways an efficient reader differs from an inefficient reader.


2. Briefly write the main ideas of the chapter here.


3. List the five steps to improving your reading found at the beginning of the chapter.

## ANSWERS: Vocabulary of Reading Quiz

1. Your eye is stopped to read
2. Understanding while you are looking at the words
3. Remembering—recall is the most difficult
4. Understand
5. Auditory reassurance—saying the words to yourself while you read
6. Rereading material: unconscious regression is a waste of time, conscious regression is sometimes necessary for understanding
7. Eyes moving from the end of one line back to the beginning of the next line
8. An almost unconscious pattern of learned behavior
9. The direction of your attention
10. Same as subvocalization; see Answer 5
11. The area your eye can see when it's fixated
12. Part of the process of replacing old habits with new habits

## ANSWERS: Progress Check 1

Charactistics of an efficient reader:

1. Three to five times faster speed
2. Smooth, rhythmic eye motions
3. Few regressions
4. Eyes always in the right place
5. Wide span of focus
6. Reduced subvocalizations
7. Flexible, purposeful approach to various material
8. Good concentration
9. Good retention

Some main ideas of the chapter are:

1. How Do You Read?
2. Habits
3. Good Readers, How Do They Do It?

Steps to Better Reading:

1. Establish a need
2. Understand the process
3. Understand why you read slowly
4. Learn new efficient habits
5. Practice

# 3 ══════════════════ Developing Speed

This chapter gives you the tools to increase your reading speed. Before you begin the lessons, read the sub-headings of the entire chapter and consider the illustrations to find out what is expected of you.

One definition of a fast reader in Chapter 2 was someone able to read three to five times faster than the average reader. Contributing to the ability to read faster are smooth and efficient eye activities, reduced subvocalization, and reduced regressions. However good readers acquired their skills, whether by trial and error, luck, or by reading this book, they are doing something different from what you do when you read. To change your old reading habits, you need to introduce something new into your reading method that invites the good habits of efficient readers to take over and supplant your old, inefficient habits.

## SOME METHODS OF INCREASING SPEED

You may be familiar with alternative methods for increased speed and comprehension, such as thinking about reading faster and/or using reading machines.

### Thinking About Reading Faster

This approach yields only limited success. If you have ever tried to make yourself read faster this way, you have placed yourself in the double bind of trying to think about the reading process while reading. It is analogous to trying to stand on a ball and balance an elephant on your head. Sooner or later, one activity gives way to the other. Usually, you wind up pronouncing the words when thinking about reading as you try to read.

When you try to move your eyes faster, unaided by some sort of pacing mechanism, you encounter an almost overwhelming physical obstacle. Several tiny muscles in each eye are working while you read. One pair of muscles is cantilevered through each side of your skull. The control required to move each one of these muscles in harmony, let alone more quickly, moves in and out of the realm of subconscious activity. Conscious attempts to manipulate these muscles by simply moving your eyes faster usually result in giving you a headache, along with minimal improvement in speed and comprehension.

### Reading Machines

Reading machines have been an interesting addition to school reading labs and to some speed reading courses. One reason they have attained some popularity is because they are fun. However, reading machines have a limited use in teaching speed reading and are very costly. Considering their limited impact on reading speeds and their high price, they are not generally cost effective. In addition, they are impractical because they cannot go with you everywhere you read. Even if you did find the funds to purchase one, they tend to be very cumbersome and require set-up and take-down time. If it is necessary to change speeds on reading machines, you must adjust some sort of dial. When you stop attending to the material on the page to make this adjustment you break your concentration.

The major argument against reading machines is that for all of the flashing lights and pretty color-coded accoutrements, they are primarily reading crutches; they do not teach a skill. To the contrary, their operation is a skill separate from the process of speed reading. Therefore, take away the machine and you have taken away whatever skill is acquired. That is, gains in speed that you may realize with a reading machine will be quickly lost when you leave the machine.

### Your Hand

The solution to reading faster is simple: use your hand to make yourself read faster. The best tool for implementing the skills of an efficient reader is *your hand, used as a pacer on the page*. Your hand on the page will guide and pace your eyes across the lines of print, adjust your speeds according to the type and difficulty of the material, and thereby eliminate or reduce your inefficient reading habits. Remember that the desire to read is essential, but desire alone will not make you read faster. If that were the case, you would be able to read as fast as necessary right now. You can make yourself read faster by using your hand as a pacer because it has all the elements of a successful tool of speed reading. It is simple, it is always with you, and it can, with practice, become an extremely effective tool with which to raise your reading speeds.

To use your hand as a pacer, underline each line on the page from margin to margin. This pacing gives your eyes a definite point of focus on the page. Your eyes are compelled to follow your finger and not wander all over the page. Since your eyes are compelled to follow your finger, unnecessary regression is almost

eliminated. Eliminating unconscious rereading of material already comprehended is an immediate and gratifying change in your reading speed.

Moreover, as your eyes are drawn more quickly along the lines of print, they
will begin to take in more words. Practicing will allow you to see more words per
fixation because your eyes are required to follow your finger at higher rates than
you are used to. This practicing stretches and expands your field of usable focus.

When you use your hand to pace yourself, speed changes can be made
smoothly and automatically, with little or no break in concentration. Because
your eyes are following a smooth and rhythmic hand motion, they tend to
smooth out their fixation and saccade patterns. Also, you will have more control
over the rhythm of your eye motions. Your return sweeps will improve because
your eyes follow your pacer to the proper point at the beginning of the new line,
rather than wandering around the page. To illustrate:

Have a friend stand in front of you and direct him or her to follow an imaginery circle
approximately six feet in diameter with his or her eyes. The actual path of the eyes
would look something like this:

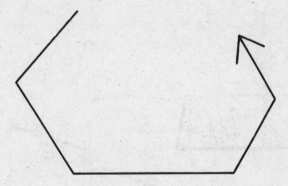

Ask the same friend to follow your hand as it makes a circle approximately six feet in
diameter. The path of your friend's eyes will look like this:

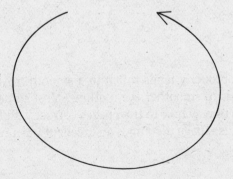

## PREPARING TO READ FASTER

Before you learn to use your hand to read faster, you must learn two preparatory steps.

### Breaking in a Book

Breaking in a book is the first thing to do in getting ready to read faster. Most paperback or new hardback books have stiff pages. You don't want to struggle with the pages while trying to learn new speed reading techniques. Therefore, place the book with its spine on the table as illustrated. Beginning with the first and last 20 or so pages of the book, press them flat against the front and back cover. Keep going until you reach the middle of the book. This step will save your books from an early retirement because it stresses the spine evenly so the book's pages do not fall out. Breaking in a book properly also flairs out the pages so that next step can be more easily accomplished.

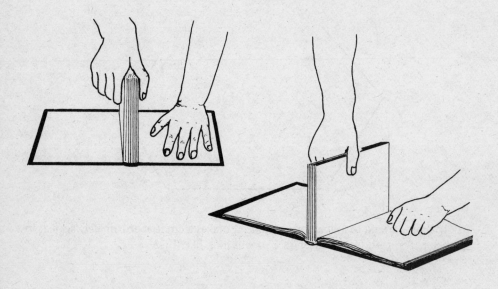

### Turning Pages

Turning pages properly lends much to a smooth, rhythmic hand motion, which, in turn, leads to smoother eye motions. Most students express surprise when told they don't know how to turn pages correctly. But there *is* an efficient way to turn pages. Also, page turning is an excellent warm-up activity before the practice exercises. Some aspects of the drills that follow are purely physical, and, like any physical exercise, it's best to spend some time warming up mentally and physically before attempting the main exercise.

### Left-Handed People

If you are left-handed you will use your left hand to pace yourself, so you will turn pages with your right hand. Be ready, when your left hand completes the bottom line on the right side of the page, to quickly and smoothly turn the page. Then your left hand can quickly and smoothly go on pacing your eyes on the next page. If you use your left hand to pace yourself *and* turn pages, you will break the rhythm of the hand motion and invite a break in your concentration.

### Right-Handed People

If you are right-handed, page turning is a bit more complicated. Place your left hand at the top of the left page with your thumb and index finger extending over onto the right page to hold that page down. (See illustration.) Use your right hand to pace yourself as you read. Slip your left index finger under the right page so that when you come to the bottom of the right page, you can quickly and smoothly flip the page with your left index finger. Then your eyes can readily move to the first line of the new page. Practice these activities for a few minutes so they are done properly. They will feel strange at first, but with practice, will become second nature. Keep in mind that it will be increasingly important that you turn pages correctly as you move to higher speeds. Practice this new skill and learn it well from the start. Try page turning for one minute, then try the following page turning exercise.

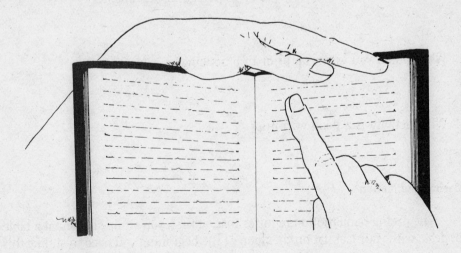

## Page Turning Exercise

This exercise lets you feel comfortable turning pages a new way and is also a good warm-up for the beginning of each practice session.

1. Sit at a table or desk with your book flat on the table.

2. Mark off sixty pages (with paper clips) in a book of your choice. (Hardbound books are the easiest to start with as they do not move all over the table as you do this exercise.)

3. Your goal is to turn all sixty pages in one minute, one page per second. Most students look at us as if we just told them to eat dirt the first time we tell them of this goal. This is normal. Our answer to their quizzical look is that many times during the course, they will want to give us that type of look, but will find that they really can do the exercise after all.

4. After you have turned sixty pages, increase your goal to seventy.

## Progress Check 1

1. When you use your hand as a pacer, you give your eyes everything *except* which of the following:

   a. a definite point of focus

   b. reduced regressions

   c. a narrower span of focus

   d. smoother eye motions

   e. more efficient return sweeps

2. Why do you need to turn pages as described in this chapter?



3. Why should you warm up prior to practicing?



4. What activity is a good warm-up?



## Basic Hand Motion

The pacing hand motion requires that, at first, you sit up straight at a table or desk, with your feet flat on the floor. At the beginning you need to sit like this to simplify learning the skill. Later you may use this hand motion wherever you like.

Use your writing hand index finger. (This distinction is made because some people are ambidextrous.) Underline each line of print from margin to margin with your index finger. (See illustration.) Your eyes should follow your finger along the lines of print. Move your finger along the line slowly enough to understand, but don't let your finger stop. Use a light touch. You need not hover over the page with your pacing finger, but don't drag your finger too heavily or you might wind up with words on it.

When your finger reaches the end of the line, perform a return sweep with your finger and your eyes. Remember, a return sweep is simply the motion that gets your eyes back to the first word of the next line, ready to read.

An interesting situation develops with return sweeps. As your eyes perform the return sweeps, they are theoretically between two lines of print and moving backwards. Not much information is contained between the lines, so movement backwards is often a temptation for your eyes to wander over the page. Some reading experts estimate that as much as 20 percent of your reading time is spent performing return sweeps. People are usually dismayed to learn that if they read for five hours last week, one hour was spent between the lines, moving backwards. To counteract the tendency to dawdle on return sweeps, do the following: take as much time as you need to read, underlining the lines from left to right, but when you reach the end of the line, pick your finger up slightly and move it back quickly to the first word of the next line, ready to read; this greatly reduces your eyes' tendency to wander.

**Exercises for Basic Hand Motion**

Always remember, this hand motion is not magic. There is no deep secret about how to read faster. It is simply an improvement of a physical skill that can be acquired through instruction and practice, just as any other physical skill can be improved, from riding a bicycle to skiing. To learn it, you must practice it correctly and consistently.

Keep the motion of your hand pivoting from your elbow rather than your wrist. (See figure above.) Notice that the wrist is not bent. You should move from the elbow rather than the wrist for two reasons. First, your wrist tires much sooner than your elbow, as those of you who are tennis players will confirm. Second, if you pivot from the wrist, you tend to get an arching motion with your finger that is not conducive to underlining the straight line on the page. Most people who pivot from the wrist do so because they are resting their forearms on the table. The best way to avoid this is to move the book (which is flat on the desk) closer to your body. This will move your forearm away from the table. You will probably find that the closer you move the book to your body, the more you will want to tilt the book, left side down. (Opposite tilt for left-handed people). Notice the tilt in the illustration again. This is fine, and in fact, is beneficial to your eyes because it gives them a chance to change focus a bit as they move along the lines of print.

The best way to introduce yourself to this hand motion is to turn the following article upside-down, so you're looking at the print upside-down and your mind can focus exclusively on the hand movements.

Now in the following section, try the new hand motion with your book upside-down for a minute or two. Remember to keep your page-turning hand ready to turn to the next page as smoothly and quickly as you can when you reach the bottom of the page. After practicing for a few minutes with the print upside-down, turn it rightside-up and read the section using your new hand motion.

## Reading Selection

There are 1,616 total words in this article. Read the entire article with your basic step and time yourself to see how long it takes. About half-way through the article, stop reading and check to see if you are doing the hand motion correctly:

|  | Yes | No |
|---|---|---|
| Your other hand is poised to turn the page: | ____ | ____ |
| You are moving from margin to margin with your index finger: | ____ | ____ |
| Not stopping your finger but moving slowly enough to understand; | ____ | ____ |
| Using a light touch; | ____ | ____ |
| Pivoting from elbow rather than wrist; | ____ | ____ |
| Lifting your finger slightly on the return sweep. | ____ | ____ |

After you have finished the article, compute your words per minute; (total time it took you to read divided into 1,616 (total number of words)) and check yourself for comprehension by answering the questions following the article.

## *Jeans in the board room*
# Collegial Tone Typifies New-Style Corporation

BY JAMES FLANIGAN
*Times Staff Writer*

There is no executive dining room at the Dallas headquarters of Texas Instruments Inc., world's largest manufacturer of semiconductors with $3.2 billion in annual sales. From Chairman Mark Shepherd Jr. on down, the entire staff eats in the same large, open cafeteria, where iced tea is the strongest, and most popular, drink.

At Palo Alto-based Hewlett-Packard Co., world leader in electronic instruments, with annual sales of $2.3 billion, the office of Chief Executive John A. Young is an 8-by-10-foot area with a linoleum-covered floor, set apart by two glass partitions.

At Intel Corp. in Santa Clara, the $660 million sales, 12-year-old pioneer in microcomputing, the chief executive wears an open-neck shirt and a gold chain. Many of the employees are less formally attired—in jeans.

Those are a few of the signposts of the new American way of business management. Superficial, almost faddish in themselves, the informality and egalitarianism are indicative of a deeper commitment among the forward-looking in business to create a new style of management.

The focus on the individual is part of a reaction against what many perceive—justly or otherwise—to be the drawbacks of the largest, most outwardly successful U.S. companies. Only 20 years ago, such companies—General Motors, U.S. Steel, Exxon and the like—were viewed as wise and powerful. Now many of them are looked upon as tired bureaucracies, less responsive to change or the public, less competitive in the world and led by risk-avoiding rather than risk-taking management. Thus they are seen as less attractive places for bright young people to work.

The irony is that those companies were once small. They owe their success to having moved fast into new markets, to having found ways to motivate their employees, to having reacted quickly to competitive challenges through the years. But as the pace of world markets has quickened, critics say, the giant companies' layers of management—assistant vice presidents, senior vice presidents, executive vice presidents—have slowed their reaction time. "It takes 14 months to get a decision out of General Electric," says one entrepreneur who supplies the big company.

To combat such inertia, and yet allow small companies to grow to a size sufficient to raise capital and supply global markets, business is trying new management methods. And the effort is seen by some analysts as offering signficant promise for renewing the competitive edge of American industry.

Most of these new management styles revolve around attempts to give greater responsibility to managers and professionals throughout the organization—to achieve a collegiality as opposed to a structure of bosses and employees. The idea of dispersing responsibility and accommodating the talents of the individual responds to the reality of modern America with its highly educated, diverse work force.

At the same time, the effort mirrors, at the executive and professional levels, experiments being tried among industrial workers on the assembly lines. General Motors' quality-of-work-life program, for example, is built around giving its factory workers more say in how their work is organized and performed.

In an auto plant or electronics laboratory, under these approaches, the worker, of whatever rank or status, sets the work goals in combination with management, and then is responsible for fulfilling the goals. "You justify your existence," is how one man who knows the environment at Texas Instruments puts it.

This is a change from the attitudes of 20 years ago. Then, the image of the American business executive was the faceless, soulless "Organization Man" that William H. Whyte wrote about. The organization man was subservient to the institution; the organization man took his identity from the company, which dictated even his private life.

Today all that is changing. The new ideal is a two-way street, with the company trying to accommodate the creativity of the individual while he or she contributes that creativity to the company. The goal is to retain the spirit of the small, entrepreneurial company—aggressive, willing to take risks, alive to changing opportunities—inside a big corporation. The spare, functional trappings—in contrast to the monumental buildings, pile carpeting and elegant furnishings of the more traditional corporate giants—allow the individual to stand out, unobscured by the pomp of the institution.

Small business and entrepreneurship courses are crowded at major business schools. At a time when a chorus of conventional wisdom decries the decline of the American work ethic, hundreds of Americans are setting up their own businesses, dissatisfied with the pace and stratification within large companies.

"If I have an idea, I don't want some vice president asking me for a report on it in two weeks. I want action now," says 35-year-old entrepreneur Philip Drayer. (Drayer has just started his own electronics service firm in Dallas and is working seven days a week to make it go.)

"Creativity comes from the top; bureaucracy destroys creativity," says

James Treybig, who founded Tandem Computers Inc. in Cupertino, Calif., in 1974. Every Friday afternoon there is what amounts to a beer party for customers, suppliers and employees to get together at Tandem's headquarters. Unconventional, yes; bureaucratic, no.

Hewlett-Packard's Executive Vice President Dean Morton understands what Treybig is trying to do—keep communication flowing. "It's hard to move from an environment where everybody knew one another to one of 55,000 employees," Morton says. "It's hard to perpetuate values." One way H-P tries to keep thinking small is to give individual executives responsibility for segments of its business, ranging between $40 million and $250 million in annual sales.

"The world is not just filled with entrepreneurs," Intel's Grove explains. "The world is filled also with organizational types, who like to run larger and larger aggregations of people. We need both those types, and so we have a career path for the organization specialist and another for the person who likes to run a small business. You tell me what kind of person you are, and we'll find the job that suits you."

At Texas Instruments, management concluded that it is folly to take productive scientists and make them administrative vice presidents, running other scientists but no longer doing the lab work they enjoyed. But the rank of vice president or above seemed the only way to award status and pay for jobs well done. TI's solution was to create an alternative career path of fellows and senior fellows, persons continually engaged in the scientific work they enjoy but receiving the same pay and status as their colleagues in the finance, marketing and administrative ranks.

But if the old-fashioned way erred on the side of bureaucratic authority, will the new lead to self-indulgence? Hardly. The typical meeting at Texas Instruments still involves a young engineer in a darkened board room projecting charts and graphs on three giant screens in order to defend an idea or the stage of progress in a program before a tough, skeptical management who must allocate limited resources.

There are no memos, only immediate and personal contact. If successful, the engineer gets a nod and increased responsibility on the next program; if unsuccessful, a blunt, quick chewing out followed by advice and the invitation to report back in a week. Admonition, then redemption. The intent, says a top TI executive, "is to motivate, not castigate."

At Intel, says Robert Noyce, one of the founders, there is "a confident environment, but not a relaxed one."

This is just the kind of approach called for a decade ago by Peter F. Drucker, regarded by many as the nation's foremost authority on management. "What the business enterprise needs is a principle of management that will give full scope to individual strength and responsibility, as well as common direction to vision and effort," he wrote in his master text, "Management."

In his latest book, "Managing in Turbulent Times," he takes up the cry again. "The employee in most companies, and even more in most public service institutions, is basically 'underemployed,'" Drucker writes. "His responsibility does not match his capacity. He is given money instead of the status that only genuine responsbility can confer."

But with more responsibility, do we get employee management? No, says Drucker. "It is not democracy. It is citizenship."

Those seem strong terms for something traditionally thought of as a job, and for organizations thought to be in business just to make a profit. But the understanding of what a job entitles one to, and how a profit is achieved, is changing—at least among some corporations.

Hewlett-Packard, for example, has no long-term debt. Is that merely a financial preference? No, says Morton, it is part of a strategy to guarantee H-P's people continuity of employment. Morton explains that an early decision by management that the company would not periodically take on and then lay off employees "led us to avoid government contracts because of gyrations in that market and led us also to base our company on 5,000 different products so we are not dependent on any one." In other words, this highly successful company says that the motive force for its business strategy involved its employees—not the stockholders, or the market.

Such management methods

don't work for small or medium-sized companies. They appear to work for a very large, highly successful U.S. company—perhaps the most successful of the postwar era: International Business Machines Corp. There also are no layoffs at IBM.

Arjay Miller, recently retired dean of Stanford's Business School and one-time president of Ford Motor Co., calls International Business Machines Corp. the best-managed company in the country. "They haven't canned anybody since 1935 except for cause," Miller says. "Yet they have great creative tension. They encourage competition among their people. Wild ducks, old Tom Watson called them...."

"Wild geese" is actually what the late Thomas Watson Sr., who built IBM, called them, but the meaning is clear: IBM gives its people strong guidance but also responsbility to follow their ideas. Then it gives them the security of knowing they won't be out on the street if the idea doesn't work or the economy turns down.

It may be an accident of history or geography, but there is no monument anywhere called The IBM Building. As at TI, H-P and Intel, the Armonk, N.Y., headquarters of IBM is a group of unpretentious, low-slung buildings. To some analysts, it is a sign that IBM, with its $23 billion in annual sales, still knows how to think small.

## Comprehension Questions

Write T or F on the line provided for the following true or false questions:

_____ 1. The outward casual appearance reflects on inward commitment to a new management style.

_____ 2. The perspective of business, according to the author, has moved from the individual to the larger conglomerate.

_____ 3. One major effort of new management is to endow managers and professionals with more responsibility.

_____ 4. According to the author, the evolution of the importance of the individual in large corporations is largely a one-way street.

_____ 5. The author maintains that emphasis on the individual will probably lead to an era of self-indulgence in business.

## STUDENTS' QUESTIONS AND CONCERNS

Interspersed throughout this chapter are typical students' questions and concerns that seem to appear in every class. They are valid and indicate that a student is serious about learning a new skill. These, by no means, include all questions posed, but they do represent the majority of student concerns when the new skill is introduced.

*Question/Concern: Isn't pointing a reading habit I was supposed to get rid of in elementary school?* The first step to faster reading is to apply your hand to the page. That canot be all, however, because some very poor readers use their hands to read. In fact, some of our best students object because they have unpleasant memories of elementary school teachers forbidding them to use their hands to read. In the case of an immature reader, the elementary school teachers have a good argument: the evidence of maturing readers in the first and second grade is for them not to feel the need to point to and say each word. The situation is entirely different in our case, but the old rubric still persists. Don't worry, your second grade teacher is not going to scold you now for putting your hand on the page.

*Question/Concern: Where should I be looking?* Look at the words right above your finger as it moves along the lines of print.

Most people tend to look at their finger when they begin this new skill. In fact, your eyes may act as if your finger was the most fascinating thing ever seen. This is normal and will stop as soon as you become bored with your finger and decide to view the words. Some people discover that their eyes race ahead of the finger or that their finger is ahead of their eyes. This, too, is normal and simply requires practice to develop the new eye/hand coordination necessary for this skill.

## PRACTICE WITH YOUR NEW SKILL

The next thing is to use a systematic method to read. It is insufficient to simply move your hand along the lines of print because your old habits are too firmly ingrained into your reading behavior to change that easily. You must now practice at word rates far exceeding your present ability to comprehend. A key point to remember is that practicing is *not* the same as reading. You now need to practice at very high rates to develop eye/hand coordination and to break your old, inefficient eye patterns. If you could graph the realtionships between your reading and practice rates and how they affect your comprehension, it would look like the graph on page 45.

The speeds on the graph are approximate, but the pattern of speed/ comprehension function is the same for anyone wishing to read faster. The first emphasis is on speed, and with this initial push for speed, comprehension drops substantially. After practicing at high speeds, the drop back to a comfortable

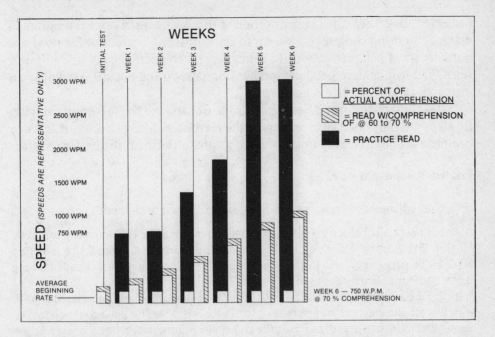

speed usually is higher than the original speed, and comprehension consequently rises.

The change in speeds and relative comprehension is the same experience you might have on a highway. When you first enter, things on the highway seem quite fast and for some people, a little out of control with regard to perceiving everything along the highway. After a short time, however, you acclimate to the speed, and it may then seem that you are moving slower than you really are. When you leave the highway, there is sometimes the floating sensation of slow motion related to the way your brain is adjusting to the flow of information to it. Those noticeable speeding up and slowing down sensations are short lags your brain experiences before adjusting to the change of the speed of the information. The amazing thing is that your brain does it with great ease.

You can take this same adaptability and apply it to reading faster with your hand as a pacer. *By constantly raising the ceiling of your practicing rate, you raise the level of speed that you can read with good comprehension.* The exercises in this book are designed to raise your pacing and reading speeds.

## COMPREHENSION VS. SPEED

Speed *must* be the first emphasis of skill development. Comprehension will suffer in the beginning, and that is expected. In fact, if you feel *too* comfortable with your comprehension, you are going too slowly. To move your eyes out of the old patterns, you must push your eyes along to speeds that preclude satisfying comprehension. This does not mean to say that comprehension is to be neglected altogether. The greater portion of this book's instructional program is designed to bring comprehension up to standards you desire. But for now, you must let go of comprehension (to some degree) to address your new physical skills. You *will* achieve good comprehension later in the book *if* you follow all instructions and practice diligently.

Read "Practicing Your New Skill" (page 61) and try the following exercise. Do steps 1-8 only once for now. Repeat the exercise as many times as it takes to complete an hour of daily practice after you have finished this entire chapter.

**Practice Reading Exercise**

You will need: a book, paper clips, timer, pencil and paper.

1. Choose a hardback book that you have already read or that is relatively simple for this first exercise. Hardback books simplify page turning and print size is better. Mark off 60 pages anywhere in the book with paper clips. Using correct page-turning technique, turn all sixty pages in one minute.

2. Find a good place in the book to begin your practice. Mark your starting point with a paper clip and read for one minute with your Basic Step for good comprehension. Remember to turn pages correctly. At the end of one minute, underline the last line you completed reading. Compute your words per minute (see Appendix A for directions on how to compute words per minute). Record the words per minute at the top of your paper and circle it.

3. From where you stopped reading, count two times (2 x) as many pages as you read the first time into new material and put a clip on the last page of the selection. You now have a section in which to practice. Your goal is to move through the section with your Basic Step in one minute. Your first priority is to reach your paper clip: your second priority is to see as much as you can. After the one minute is up and you have reached your mark, write down anything you remember seeing: isolated words, numbers, etc.

4. Add two more pages to the section you just did. Read with your Basic Step for as good comprehension as you can for one minute. You will be looking at part of the previous section (try to see something new) plus two new pages. Add to your list after you have read.

5. Move your paper clips over two new pages and drop one old page of the section. Get through the section with your Basic Step in one minute. Add to your list.

6. Add two new pages to the section and drop one old page. Read for one minute; write.

7. Add three new pages and drop one old page. Read for one minute; write.

8. Mark with a paper clip that point in the section where comprehension was totally lost and read for as much comprehension as you want for three minutes. Compute your words per minute and compare to your first circled words per minute. You may wish to record these speeds in the back of the book.

9. Repeat steps 2-7 in new material until you have practiced for 50 minutes.

## READING

Reading means understanding as stipulated in the beginning of the lessons, but since it is such an important concept, we redefine it. Understanding printed words means more than simply pronouncing as you move your eyes along the lines. Reading means understanding the things, concepts, and ideas symbolized on the page by tiny black marks.

## PRACTICE READING

Practice reading means going as fast as you can, getting as much as you can. First, notice that the operative word in the definition of practicing reading is "going," not reading. This distinction is of utmost importance because if you physically move your eyes across the lines as fast as you can, you won't read because you won't totally understand. That is where the second phrase comes in: "getting as much as you can." At times, "getting as much as you can" may mean that you recognize the print as the English language, but little more. If you follow the practice reading exercise directions, then getting as much as you can may mean that one or two words on the page are familiar. You were beginning to practice read with your first exercise on page 46. This is how it should be in the beginning.

Again, notice that the first and primary focus on the definition of practice reading is the "going." "Getting" comes second and is subordinate to "going." If you ever feel totally comfortable practice reading, you are going too slowly. It is essential to look at 500 words per minute before you can ever consider reading 500 words per minute.

## PRACTICE READING PAY-OFFS

The interesting thing that happens when you practice read correctly and maintain the proper speed (too fast to totally understand what is on the page) is that you begin to see more and more words. After successive practice reading sessions, you may see 10 words per page, then 15 and then many words will come together into short, understandable phrases. The progression most experience in terms of how much they see when they practice read is as follows:

1. blur
2. isolated words
3. short phrases
4. general ideas
5. all the comprehension needed.

**Progress Check**

1. Which of the following items make for a good, basic hand motion?

    \_\_\_\_a. sitting up at a table with book flat on the table

    \_\_\_\_b. chewing gum

    \_\_\_\_c. using your index finger of the hand you use to write

    \_\_\_\_d. using a light touch

    \_\_\_\_e. not touching the page

    \_\_\_\_f. lifting your finger lightly on return sweeps and quickly returning it to the first word of the next line

    \_\_\_\_g. pivoting from your elbow rather than your wrist

    \_\_\_\_h. keeping your eyes looking at your finger

2. Why is the first emphasis in skill development on speed?

3. Define reading.

4. Define practice reading.

**Reading Selection**

1. Use the following article for this exercise.

2. Read for good comprehension with your Basic Step from the beginning of the article for three minutes. Compute your words per minute.

3. Multiply your words per minute by 7. Mark off that many words from the beginning of the article. (Consider the portion you have already read as a running start.)

9 words per line in the article

$N$ = the number of words in your section

$N/9$ = the number of lines to mark off

4. Your goal is to practice read that section in one minute. Practice reading means going as fast as you can, getting as much as you can, and no where will this be more apparent to you than in this section. Your finger will be a blur and you may accidentally skip a line or two, or you may hit some lines twice if you are doing the exercise correctly. This is to be expected. Your first priority is to make your mark. If you don't, set your timer and try again until you can make your mark.

## *Late start*

# GM: A Giant Awakening to Wider World

BY JAMES FLANIGAN
*Times Staff Writer*

DETROIT—The words of Alex C. Mair, head of technical staffs at General Motors Corp. and therefore a very high-ranking executive, are momentarily arresting. But the sentiment is quickly, and sadly, familiar.

"I can tell you that 20 years ago if you asked anybody who was the leading automobile company in the world, everybody would have said Chevrolet and it was true. People from foreign automobile companies would come to look at our plants and our engineering.

"Recently, though, we've been going to see how they do it. We go to Japan . . . ."

What changed? Mair has no real answer. But he tries to lay blame on an amorphous decline of the national spirit. "It's a national thing," he says. "We got rich enough to decide not to be the best."

Mair's gloom is excessive. Unfortunately, Detroit at bay is like a man depressed—can't believe there's anybody happy in the world. But just as the currently fashionable mourning over the terminal ills of American in-dustry is premature, so Detroit's view of the national spirit is more alibi than accurate.

For what may be true of GM and the auto industry is not true of IBM and the computer industry, of Boeing and airplanes, of Dow and chemicals, of Caterpillar Tractor or General Electric or Procter & Gamble. It is not true of Intel and the U.S. electronics industry, of Citicorp. and international banking, of Fluor Corp. and worldwide engineering or, for that matter, of Levi Strauss and the universal business of blue jeans.

American companies hold the leading edge of technology in pharmaceuticals, biosciences, telecommunications and practically everything to do with oil and natural gas. From environmental science to agricultural know-how, America leads the world.

Still, there is trouble in the car business. Chrysler needed a bailout, Ford has been losing a bundle in this country and even General Motors is in the red so far this year. The nation is understandably worried. It is all very well to say, as experts do, that within 20 years electronics will be the country's largest industry. The car business, directly or indirectly employing one in every six persons in the labor force, is the largest industry today.

When it fails to deliver the goods, the typically American reaction asks, "Who's to blame?" And when executives in Detroit respond by blaming the customers, the government or assorted foreigners—everybody but themselves—it only heightens the public anxiety.

The truth is that both critics and carmakers are caught up in the process of America once again awakening to a wider world. The unfamiliar and uncomfortable realization that America's economy is linked with the rest of the world is brought home every day by rising oil prices or sinking dollar values. Was it only yesterday that the approved American response to foreign currency was to ask "How much is that in real money?"

The current alarm is over industrial competitiveness. Today's cry is, "How come the Japanese seem to do things better?" All perspective is lost and the nation becomes hypochondriac. We have seen this before. Thirty years ago serious men asked "Who lost China?" as if the world's most populous country had slipped through an infielder's glove. A decade ago the inquisition asked who got us into Vietnam, and why? The true picture usually takes a while to emerge.

And the true picture of General Motors, for one, is that of an awakening giant. In recent years, GM has been doing the right things.

It may not admit publicly that it made mistakes, but internally it has been saying by its actions that past policies did not measure up and new ones must be tried. For nine years it has been quietly reforming its personnel policies, specifically working on the quality of work life at its assembly plants where absenteeism gets up to 12% of the work force on any given day and 30% on Mondays.

For seven years it has been downsizing its gas-guzzling automobiles, bringing out cars like the Chevrolet Chevette and Citation—the largest-selling cars in the United States this year and last—and the Cadillac Seville, which runs neck and neck in sales with all 11 models of the luxury invader, Mercedes.

For the last two years it has been making an open effort to finally be a true competitor on the only market that exists today—the global market. GM is transforming itself from a company dominant in the United States, with international efforts best described as afterthoughts, into a worldwide supplier of cars.

GM is undeniably late in making all of these changes and had to be pushed by the government into some of them. It has become international-minded in the last two years, whereas multinational companies have been developing for more than 20 years. It seems odd that it makes the largest-selling small cars but lacks the capacity to make as many as the market demands.

Change is hard, and it is especially so for a company like GM because flaws must be acknowledged in a management system that used to be called a model. To understand what happened one must step back and see just what General Motors is and what it means to the industrial history of the world.

First of all, it is big—the world's largest manufacturing company. GM's $66.3 billion in sales last year was greater than the combined sales of the top four foreign carmakers: Fiat, Volkswagen, Renault and Toyota. GM's $2.9 billion net income was almost three times the combined profits of Volkswagen, Toyota and Nissan—maker of Datsuns. (Fiat and Renault lost money.) GM's 853,000 employees equaled the combined totals of VW, Renault, Toyota and Nissan (although the Japanese company employment figures are absurdly low because of a different method of calculation). GM, until this year, produced more cars than the entire Japanese industry. The company is determined to recover that distinction.

It has the capital for an epic battle. GM last year paid its shareholders $1.5 billion in dividends and still generated $4.6 billion for reinvestment in the business. It is spending $40 billion over the next five years to establish clearly its supremacy in the world automobile industry.

The numbers seem daunting, but not everybody is daunted by numbers. Hideo Sigiura, executive vice president of Honda Motor Co., was quoted recently as saying: "The amount of money they are spending really doesn't bother me. In any country the quality of products and the productivity of workers depend on management.

When Detroit changes its management system, we'll see more powerful American competitors."

Strong words, and attacking GM's special pride—its management system. Before GM was a leading maker of cars it had to become a triumph of management science—the modern discipline that author Peter F. Drucker calls the most significant contribution of this century to the history of the world, and that Harvard Business School historian Alfred D. Chandler Jr. calls the unique American contribution to the world.

The methods by which professional managers organize and guide enormous, far-flung economic enterprises have developed only in the last century. Yet they are taken for granted today. Business management was much more catch-as-catch-can when the modern GM was formed in 1920.

At that time, General Motors was five entrepreneurial companies, each investing in its own way, pulling in its own direction. The lack of organization almost brought the lot into bankruptcy in the postwar slump of 1920. Members of the DuPont family, of Delaware and chemicals, and a 45-year-old engineer named Alfred P. Sloan Jr. organized modern GM out of that chaos.

Sloan, who died in 1966, told in his book, *My Years With General Motors,* how he struck a balance by devising a central office to control the five semi-autonomous divisions. In that way the company benefited from the independent thinking and market knowledge of the divisional managers, but was preserved as a single entity because a central management apportioned capital and set long-term policy. An accounting master named Donaldson Brown, who came to GM from DuPont, developed an intricate system of financial controls, assigning to each division an expected return on investment, depending on its special circumstances.

This system of differential expectations fit right into the grand strategy that Sloan perfected later in the 1920s—that of five different car makes, selling in five different price ranges, to meet what he perceived to be a national market segmented by income and taste. We know the five, of course, as Chevrolet, Pontiac, Oldsmobile, Buick and Cadillac. The company made more money on each Cadillac but sold fewer of them, less money on each Chevrolet but sold them in great volume.

Sloan read the market right. By 1926 GM passed Ford in sales and was never after that less than America's No. 1 automobile company. Henry Ford had provided the Model T, a basic, low-cost vehicle. Ford had pitched his strategy to making the Model T lower-priced and simpler as production volumes rose. But the market moved away from him to the higher-priced GM cars, which offered style and color. It was a lesson the world automobile business never forgot.

Of course, GM cemented its dominance by more than styling. In the 1930s, the great technical innovations all came from GM: The high-compression engine, the automatic transmission (introduced widely after World War II), the front-end suspension which made for the comfortable rides that became synonymous with American cars. GM developed anti-knock gasoline and durable paint finishes and adapted the diesel engine to automotive use.

Is it any wonder that GM was the model corporation Drucker wrote about in 1945 in his pioneering book on management, *"Concept of a Corporation"?* GM'S superior organization and production abilities had helped win the war; it was the very symbol of American success.

But by the late 1950s Drucker was no longer calling GM the model, because it was not changing as the world was changing. Today the Austrian-born management expert is impatient with most criticism of GM, finding it superficial. But he does identify two basic mistakes. One is that the company "has been dead from the neck up in public relations" since the 1937 sit-down strikes, when the United Auto Workers occupied a GM plant until the company agreed to negotiate recognition of the union.

Public relations may seem like a small thing, but GM's grand opacity in speaking about itself may have hurt it in several subtle ways—most notably in its response to the rise of consumerism in the 1960s. The company today is bending great efforts to attract the brighter young graduates to work for it. It must convince them, says Alex Mair, that exciting work is going on at GM. The years of poor public image make that difficult.

But the other mistake cited by Drucker is far more central and serious. It is nothing less, he says, than "a grievous and total misreading of the world economy." After the war, following some debate on whether the company should even bother, GM resuscitated Adam Opel AG, the German automobile company it had acquired in 1927. But from that time until 1978 it left Opel to run pretty much as a German car company, with overseers sent out from Detroit. It did not integrate its international and domestic businesses. As Drucker puts it, if an executive was sent to Opel it did not mean a promotion, it meant he had missed out on the big jobs. Those were in Detroit.

In contrast to Ford, GM brought no Europeans into its management structure. GM played Fortress America just at the time when far-sighted corporations like IBM were developing talent of whatever nationality to work in the global market.

The most successful automobile company outside the United States today is Ford, not GM. It is Ford because during the 1960s, Arjay Miller, then president of Ford, integrated the company's domestic and international operations—precisely the move made by GM in 1978. Miller, recently retired as dean of Stanford University's Business School, recalls that time:

"When I became president, you had Ford of Germany and Ford of England. But I set up Ford of Europe. It was a move questioned by GM and the industry but it was a good idea. We got a common body and it took a hell of a lot of cost out by having a common car for Ford in Europe."

Miller went beyond that. He abolished Ford's international division, the corporate pigeonhole in which all "foreign" matters were dealt with. "It became clear to me that the toughest problems were in international but they were working with the second team," he says. "The U.S. finance guy was better than the international guy, the U.S. marketing guy better than the foreign and so forth. We just eliminated that separation."

It was a move of good management. The result today is that Ford's international operations are making the profits that are saving the company, which is losing money domestically.

But because of the lack of such a management move—"In all candor, we haven't been as good in the international area as our competition," says current GM chairman Thomas A. Murphy—GM's perspective was skewed so that it failed to adapt to changed market circumstances back home in the States. One failing, in short, led to another.

In the 1950s and '60s the great growth markets for the automobile were in Europe and Japan. Restrictions held GM and other American manufacturers out of the Japanese market but GM's own inactivity prevented it from taking full advantage of the other. It missed out on the growth markets.

Consider these numbers: From 1946, the year after World War II ended, through 1955, GM's unit sales of cars and trucks manufactured in the U.S. and Canada grew 20% a year on average. But from 1956 through 1979, its unit sales in the domestic market grew about 4% a year on average.

Meanwhile, overseas unit sales—mainly Britain, Germany and Australia—grew 18% a year from 1956 to 1970. But GM did not build up its capacity overseas as did Ford or, for that matter, Volkswagen—which dominates Brazil and Mexico.

GM was therefore left with the U.S. market, which by 1960, with one car on the road for every three Americans, had come close to saturation. That means that car sales were, in effect, largely replacement sales. In a replacement market, a company's sales and earnings could grow with the increase in population—under 2% a year—or to the extent it could take sales from competitors or to the extent it could extract a higher per-unit price from the customer.

The last approach, an adaptation of the original Sloan marketing system, proved to be the U.S. automobile industry's strategy for the 1960s. It was called "more car per car." It is summed up pithily by a former top auto executive: "You put in a clock that costs $10 and charge $30 for it."

The overseer of the strategy at GM in the late 1950s was still Sloan himself. He remained as honorary chairman until his death, at 91, in 1966. And his influence, say those who know, discouraged fundamental changes by GM until recent years. Sloan's original strategy had read the American market—perhaps all markets—rightly. But he did not translate it to foreign markets, nor did he anticipate basic changes in the U.S. market. "Sloan was right," says Peter Drucker, "but became obsolete as everything does."

Considering the market changes of the 1960s—the rise of consumer demands for quality, the fall of Detroit's reputation for quality, the advent of the Japanese in force in the early 1970s—it has been a mystery why the management system devised by Sloan failed to respond more quickly. After all, with divisional managers attuned to day-to-day markets, and central staff looking out long range, one would have thought that GM's system was ideally prepared for change. That it responded slowly shows that systems run corporations only up to a point; human beings are the real management.

What seems to have happened is that both divisional managers and the central staff riveted their attention on the very short term. When GM executives are criticized for failing to respond to market changes during that period, their stock response is that they only served up what the public wanted. But their reference is to a scant year or two—nobody's idea of the long term.

Why was this?

Well, one reason, although not explaining all of GM's moves, could be that GM executives are awarded bonuses based on the current year's profits. These bonuses sometimes equal a year's salary. This is basic policy.

Now, no GM executive will admit to thinking short-term just because of the money. But it would be human nature to do so and the fact remains that "more car per car" was undeniably a good, money-making strategy for the short term.

High-powered "muscle" cars sold well in the 1960s. Detroit (GM with the Chevrolet Corvair) brought out its first "small" cars in 1960—to check the advance of the Volkswagen beetle—but soon caused them to grow in size, weight and expensive options.

Arjay Miller explains in terms of Ford Motor, which he led, why Detroit's automakers so long seemed to abhor the small car: "Cannibalism is the term used," Miller says. "Someone comes in to buy a Ford and they buy a Pinto—you not only make less money on the car you sell but you have to think about the profit you lose on the LTD you don't sell. There is a substitution effect. Ford and GM had to recognize the lost profit on the bigger cars they wouldn't sell if they brought out a smaller, less profitable car. It's two bites out of the apple."

Of course, a child can see that if you had a growing market you might hope to sell both small and big cars. But the U.S. automakers, GM in particular, did not have a growing market. And that made the Japanese invasion incredibly threatening.

For although Toyota, Datsun and later Honda initially offered truly small cars, their strategy emerged in the 1970s as one of offering the customer a variety of models and price ranges. The Japanese, using Sloan's original strategy, were out to displace the company Sloan had built. Every first-time Toyota buyer entered the Toyota "family" of cars, in just the way the Chevrolet purchaser traditionally entered the GM family, graduating through life and stages of income to the Cadillac. (Toyota, too, has its "Ca-

dillac," called the Crown, which it markets currently in Europe and will bring here soon. The difference in Toyota's family of cars is that all along the line they were smaller than the American automobiles. And that suited the American taste, as the 1970s brought a new emphasis to energy.)

The American carmakers had to respond, both to meet the Japanese threat and to meet U.S. fuel standards. And to its credit, GM was the company above all that did respond—starting with a decision made in 1974 to "downsize" all its cars. Thomas Murphy, who joined GM in 1938 straight out of the University of Illinois, recalls that time with emotion:

"Back in 1974, people thought the automobile industry had had it. A lot of people in the industry said the golden age had passed. But God bless him, my predecessor (Richard Gerstenberg, chairman from 1972 to 1974) made a big decision."

Murphy pauses, touches his steel-rimmed spectacles, and continues. "We made a decision at that time to bring two vehicles into our product array—the Chevette, lower in size and weight than anything we had made up to that time—and the Seville, designed to take on the Mercedes and those other luxury imports.

"And we also launched a program to remake every other vehicle we manufactured, to start at the top and take the whole thing down."

The Chevette and Seville were brought out in 18 months because they used designs already existing in Europe. Thus those cars became the genesis of a commitment by GM, isolated no more, to build a world car—a single style of automobile for every market in the world. GM's "J" cars, as they are now named, will debut next spring in the United States, in Europe and in Japan where Isuzu Motors—35% owned by GM—will carry the battle to the Japanese on their home ground.

From that standing start in 1974, GM has come far and fast. In 1975, a poor year for the business overall, Murphy, who had become chairman, kept the spending program going for GM's X-car—the designation the public knows now as the Chevrolet Citation, Pontiac Phoenix, Olds Omega and Buick Skylark.

The truth is, GM asleep at the wheel was yesterday's story. The up-to-date version is GM off the dime. Years of comparative lack of innovation now ended, every one of GM's gasoline-powered 1981 cars carries a microprocessor (microcomputer) in the engine to control fuel usage and emissions. For Japanese cars such innovations are a year or two away.

Alex Mair brings students these days to GM's sprawling Technical Center and sends them back to tell their schoolmates of the exciting engineering research going on there.

GM is spending $3 billion to build or remodel six assembly plants in the United States, $2 billion more to build new car and engine production facilities in Spain and Austria. One reason it is losing money this year is the level of expenditure to ensure its supremacy tomorrow.

This is also Murphy's retirement year. His successor has already been announced—Roger B. Smith. GM will probably report a loss for the whole year. Does that bother Murphy? "We're not in business for today, or for just tomorrow. We're in business forever."

The focus of management, once again, is on the long term.

So what of Sugiura of Honda's statement that unless Detroit changes its management system he has nothing to fear from American products? He is referring to the well-publicized higher productivity of Japanese workers compared to American factory workers (absenteeism costs GM $1 billion a year, says its personnel department).

Once again, the surprising truth is that GM has been changing its plant management practices. It is a slow process, admits Stephen Fuller, vice president for personnel administration and development. "We are trying to give people in General Motors new dimensions of responsibility, so that they will be more responsible," he says. What that means in plain English is that GM is trying to build up its employees' self-respect by showing its employees that the management respects them.

Bluntly that is it, says Fuller who was brought into GM in 1971, from Harvard, to help implement the company's quality-of-work-life program. Basically the program recognizes that the authoritarian policies that ruled their immigrant or sharecropper fathers and grandfathers will not do for today's high school-educated workers. GM, which employs hundreds of thousands, faces on another level the same problem that IBM and Hewlett Packard face with their "knowledge workers": motivation.

The company is solving the problem, Fuller explains, by breaking work units into teams of 12 or so, giving individuals more responsibility. He reports absenteeism down from 12% to 1%, scrappage rates reduced and productivity increased dramatically in plants where quality of work life has been implemented. "People do respond to good leadership," he says, "although quality of work life has nothing new in it. What is new is a recognition that given the changing nature of the work force, new approaches have to be undertaken, and the old way of managing is no longer acceptable and is totally ineffective."

He is currently bringing GM around to the recognition that layoffs during slack times are more costly than keeping the people employed. With supplementary unemployment benefits—contributed by the company—the cost of keeping the people on could be as little as 5% of pay. The cost of laying off, says Fuller, is incalculable because the good workers may not come back.

Clearly, the message is, GM is changing. And just as it takes time for the United States to adapt to a changing world, so it takes time for one of its symbolic institutions to do so. The loudly proclaimed funeral of U.S. industrial vitality will have to be postponed.

## THE "S" HAND MOTION

The other hand motion you will use is called the "S" motion. This hand motion is used primarily for practice reading and for the previewing step in the study procedure outlined in Chapter 4. It is *not* intended to be a reading hand motion, although you may find that, after some practice, you can use it to read newspaper columns and easier magazine articles.

The path of your index finger will look like this on the page:

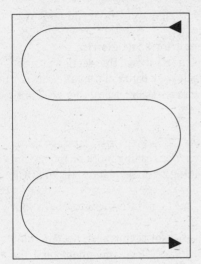 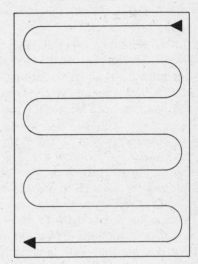

Always start the "S" motion in the upper right corner of the page and move from margin to margin. The "S" pattern can be a very fast practice reading hand motion, or you can slow it down to preview by varying the width of the pattern. The first illustration shows a fast "S" pattern that you could use for practice reading, while the second illustration shows a potential previewing "S" pattern. The adjustment of speed comes by changing the number of "cuts" or times your finger travels across the lines of print. The "S" pattern is ideal for varying your speeds because it is so easy to adjust.

Also, *unlike the Basic Step* where words per minute are directly related to your finger's speed, the "S" pattern lets you cover relatively more words per minute with less hand motion because you are spending less time per page. Therefore, most people find the "S" pattern more relaxing than the Basic Step for their practice reading.

### Exercises for the "S" Hand Motion

As your hand moves down the page, look at the area above your finger. Remember, "look" as you use this hand motion. Use this exercise in your weekly practice routine.

## Practice Reading Exercise

1. Find a hardback book for this initial practice reading exercise as the page turning will be easier.

2. Mark off 60 pages with paper clips and practice turning those pages in one minute. As you are page turning, look and try to see what the book is about.

3. Mark off a section of 3000 words in your book with paper clips.

4. Your goal is to practice read with the "S" those 3000 words in one minute. Use four or five "cuts" per page.

5. After you finish the 3000 word section, jot down any words that you remember seeing.

6. Mark off another 3000 word section and repeat the same exercise.

7. Add five pages to the section you just did and practice read that section again in one minute. Try to see something new and also reach your paper clip mark.

8. If you use this exercise for your one-hour practice session, repeat Steps 4-7 until you have practiced for 50 minutes. Break.

*Question/Concern: How can I read with the "S" since my hand is going backwards?* The "S" is *not* a reading motion; it is a *practice* reading motion. You are not expected to read backwards. Your hand is merely defining an area for your eyes to LOOK into and see as much as possible.

*Question/Concern: Where do I look with the "S"?* Look into the area above your fingers, just as you did with the basic step.

*Question/Concern: How fast should I go?* This varies for each reader. Keep in mind that *you* are your only limit as to how fast you can go. Once you understand the techniques for building your speed and you understand the progress you can make with comprehension, the speed reading skills in this book can become a life-long series of self-improvement lessons.

*Question/Concern: I feel uncomfortable doing this.* Reread Chapter 2, especially the section on "Habits." Remember, if you feel too comfortable, you are not doing the exercises correctly. This is an honest description of how you replace old, inefficient reading habits with newer, more satisfying ones. If you are uncomfortable, you have begun to threaten the old habits, the first step towards replacement. Practice is the key to comfort. Practice and time will have you feeling comfortable with your new skills.

*Question/Concern: What should my eyes be doing?* Don't worry about what your eyes are doing. You can't control the motions of your eyes and achieve good comprehension at the same time. If you have followed the explanations and directions carefully, if you have a proper page turning and hand motion going, and if you are trying to get the right type of comprehension according to the exercise's directions, then your eyes will naturally do the right things. Don't concentrate on what your eyes are doing, concentrate on what is on the page.

*Question/Concern: Everything is a blur.* At first, this is very natural. This is a radical departure for your eyes as they rapidly view lines of print. Your eyes require practice to get accustomed to this new way of sending information to your brain.

**Progress Check 3**

1. The "S" hand motion is used for:

_____a. reading

_____b. practice reading

2. You begin the "S" pattern in the:

_____a. upper right corner of the page

_____b. upper left corner of the page

3. When you are describing the "S," cuts mean:

_____a. pages

_____b. the path of your hand as it travels across the page

4. When you are using the "S" hand motion, your eyes should be:

_____a. reading backwards

_____b. reading when your hand moves from left to right and closed when your hand moves from right to left

_____c. looking into the area above your finger

5. Practice reading means _____ as fast as you can _____ as much as you can.

## APPROPRIATE PRACTICE

Practice can be either massed or distributed. Massed practice is best illustrated by those last-minute "cramming" sessions you did for finals in college. Many studies have confirmed that this type of practicing experience yields few long-lasting results for the learner. This book adheres to the distributed practice method because you are changing very tenacious habits and replacing them with new habits. Therefore, the knowledge and skills are best absorbed over a period of time, rather than in one massed practice session. Some chapters can serve as reference sections for use as particular problems appear in your practice sessions.

## REINFORCEMENT

Reinforcement can be either positive or negative, reward or punishment. We hope that you will select a reward system for your reinforcement. The results of your tests should be positive reinforcement each week.

## LEARNING CURVE AND PLATEAU

An important aspect of the instructional process is the learing curve, a visual representation of how much information you learn over a period of time. A plateau represents a stage in learning where no growth is apparent.

Such plateaus will occur in this speed reading course and in any other you encounter. Plateaus can be discouraging, but needn't be if you anticipate them and have some methods of overcoming them. Dickenson cites four reasons for plateaus in the learning curve:

1. The learner may be tired. Initially, the skills require time and effort on the part of a learner. If you are constantly tired before you begin your practice sessions or reading sessions, you will find little or no noticeable improvement in your speed or comprehension. Find another time to practice or adjust yourself in some manner so you will not become discouraged.

2. Decline in motivation. The new skills require some motivation. You may perceive the need to read faster—an internal motivation. The stack of unread, required reading on your desk may be an external motivator. Whichever the case, without some type of motivation, your learning curve will flatten out into permanent plateaus. Use positive reinforcement to get yourself going, and keep in mind that everyone's motivation lags at times. Don't give up the war because one small battle is lost. Take a moment to regroup; think about the benefits of reading faster and more efficiently.

3. Plateaus may represent a pause to rethink earlier, more simple information. The prior information may take on a whole new perspective later in the book. You will need time to integrate the information. Along with integration may come rearrangement of the earlier information for a new stage of complex learning, so give yourself some time and understanding when your speeds seem to be stuck at one level.

4. No new information is being learned, but incorrect or irrelevant information is being discarded. This process occurs when you exchange old reading habits for new ones. Often a lag occurs between the dumping of the old and the firm acquisition of the new. This may show up as a plateau.

The best way to overcome plateaus is to practice your way out of them. Reapply yourself to even more diligent practicing, and you will find yourself moving out of a plateau much sooner. The rule for plateaus is: "Don't just sit there, do something!"

## PRACTICING YOUR NEW SKILLS

Plan to spend at least a week or perhaps even 10 days practicing the skills presented in this chapter. You learn these skills by doing them, not simply reading about them. Moreover, you don't want to reinforce your old habits of reading, so read everything (except television ads and billboards) with your hand.

### Use It

To change the reading habits of a lifetime, you must practice at least 50-60 minutes a day. If you need to divide up that hour, don't divide it up into more than two half-hour sessions, otherwise the skills won't have a chance to develop adequately. The first week you practice will be the most difficult for you because your initial assault on the old habits will be met with the most resistance. Consequently, your comprehension won't be terrific at the beginning of the week, but if you practice, you will begin to feel more comfortable.

The minimum reading rate will be identified at the beginning of each week's practice exercise. The first week's minimum rate is 500 words per minute. This minimum rate will also be difficult to reach comfortably at the beginning of the week's practice, but with diligence you will notice that the minimum rate is well within your capabilities by the end of the week. Some people have started this book already reading at a rate of 400+ words per minute. Those of you with 400+ beginning speeds should raise this first week's minimum rate to 800 words per minute.

### Write It Down

After you complete an exercise, write down anything you remember. This usually consists of isolated words at the beginning of your lesson. Thus, a "laundry list" is the first step. After you have practiced, you will notice more and more words. Soon they come together into short phrases and brief ideas. Don't feel that, because you saw only a few words (the ones you can write down) per page, those words are not useful. This is simply not true, as you can see from the following exercise. In the following lists of words, how much information can

| BOOK A | BOOK B | BOOK C | BOOK D |
|--------|--------|--------|--------|
| deciduous | transaction | taxonomy | Kennedy |
| evergreen | demand | behavior | Time |
| sunny | refuse | psychomotor | Luce |
| pine | reserve | develop | editor |
| grown | 1930s | ideas | campaign |
| yew | public | program | years |
| years | open-market | essential | liberal |
| soil | $5 million | psychology | popular |

you deduce about the type of books the words came from? Check your answers with the answers at the end of the chapter.

It is interesting to note that, at first, the words you see seem to "pop out" at you. They also seem to be capitalized words, numbers, italicized words, etc., anything different from the regular lines of print.

## Why Write It Down?

You need to write after you have drilled to place yourself in a position of responsibility concerning the information (however vague) on the page. It requires you to see as much as you can. It also requires your active involvement with the material as you try to decide what is going on. Moreover, writing after you have read prepares you to improve comprehension and retention skills. Although "laundry lists" may seem very rudimentary to you now, writing them is a sound beginning toward validating your new speeds, proving that your brain is quite capable of receiving printed information at much higher speeds and retaining much more of that information.

Use the reading exercises and practice on pages 49 and 60, as well as the exercise at the end of the chapter for your hour's practicing. Use your own materials for the exercises.

*Question/Concern: How do you time yourself?* The best way to time yourself is to get a tape recorder and stop watch or a watch with a sweep second hand. Turn the tape recorder on and record yourself saying "go." Wait one minute or whatever practice pattern of timing you want and then say "stop." You can design a week's worth of practicing times and simply turn your recorder off and on to get the correct time. Sometimes it's wise to record yourself saying how long the timing is at the beginning of the drill if it is a longer time (five minutes or more). It is also a good idea to give yourself some intermittent times. "Two minutes are gone," "half your time is left," "two minutes are left," are some helpful remarks to keep your pace consistent throughout a drill.

A kitchen timer or egg timer can help you keep time as well. Your children or a friend can also help in your timing effort. Children love to scream "Stop!" and "Go!" in your ear, which tends to send you to an early grave and them to an early bedtime.

*Question/Concern: I can't find an hour a day to practice.* If you plan an hour a day for yourself now, consider how many hours you will save in the future. If you read just 50 words per minute faster in the first drill, that can be translated into 3,000 more words per hour. Those 3000 words can be roughly translated into 10 more pages of an average book per hour. That improvement comes after only a few minutes of drilling. Consider the improvement you will realize after a week's practice. If you could have read 50 words faster ten years ago, how many reading hours would that have saved you?

Even if it means a sacrifice to you now in terms of finding the time, it still is prudent to do so. You can make the rest of your life somewhat easier. How many opportunities do you have to make such a definitive improvement in your life? And at a cost of only an hour a day?

*Question/Concern: I saw only three words in the last exercise.* Three words may be a lot, considering how fast you were going. Perhaps you were only expected to see one word. That means you saw 66.6 percent more than you were expected to see! The point is, take what you did see positively and strive to see more. What can you deduce from those three words? It may be only conjecture now, but use those three words positively rather than becoming discouraged.

*Question/Concern: Why do I have to go margin to margin with my hand when I practice read? Sometimes I skip lines or hit the same line twice because I am going so fast.* At the beginning of the practice reading skills, your eyes need all the direction they can get. If you don't move from margin to margin, your eyes won't expand their field of focus as well. Neglecting margins also lends itself to the beginning of a sloppy hand motion. Don't ignore the margins; it will promote poor comprehension when you read. Don't be overly concerned about skipping lines or hitting the same line twice, as long as you strive to use the hand motion properly.

*Question/Concern: Why do you start in the right-hand corner of the page with the "S"?* Because the "S" is not a reading hand motion, you start in the upper right-hand corner to discourage reading the first line of the page. If you read the first line, you will be tempted to read every line your hand underlines as it moves from left to right, and ignore the rest of the text as your hand moves from right to left in the "S" motion.

*Question/Concern: Sometimes I look for just a word so I have something to write down. Is this a mistake?* Yes. When you practice read and limit yourself to searching for one or two words to have something to write down, you defeat the purpose of practice reading. The problem is, that when you latch onto a word, you usually say to yourself, "Good, there's at least one thing I'll be able to write down." But while you are saying that to yourself, you are not concentrating on the other words. When you come to the second word you plan to use, the first word is usually forgotten, and so on, throughout the exercise. This defeats the purpose of practice reading: getting as much as you can. The best way to get as much as you can is to relax and have confidence that you will see something because you *want* to see something. You have lost some of your auditory reassurance and therefore are looking for other types of reassurance. The best way to reassure yourself that you saw the material is to practice read and try to see as much as you can. Then let the writing afterward reassure you that you indeed, saw something.

*Question/Concern: My arm (neck, shoulder) hurts.* Most beginning students experience this. It is probably because most people don't know how to be physically relaxed while remaining mentally alert. If you try to relax your body while performing the exercises, you will soon see a relaxation of your arm (neck, shoulders). Also, as you become more familiar with the skills, you will need less of your physical energies, and hence less of your muscles, to perform the skills.

*Question/Concern: I can't understand anything.* This also must be turned into a positive statement. Even if you saw only one word, that situation can be analogous to the question, "Is the glass half empty or half full?" Because you are engaged in a new information acquisition process, you are not going to understand much at the beginning.

Since reading is such an intimate method of understanding your environment, when you do not understand, you become anxious. This is normal, and what you do with the anxiety is crucial to whether you become an effective speed reader. Some people evade the issue; they pretend nothing is wrong or that they understand, when in fact they do not. This is not a helpful reaction to learning the new skills. Other people panic. They cannot accept the ambiguity that usually evolves from the exchange of old habits for new. The great majority of people, however, learn to cope. They recognize that some work and anxiety are involved with acquiring a new skill, and they are willing to make the investment for long-term, worthwhile gains.

Find something to understand! If you have the intellectual ability to read and follow the directions in this book, you can do well with this new skill. There is nothing magic about reading faster. You merely have to improve skills you already possess. The hand, when included in the reading process, can be a means of self-discipline and internalizing new reading habits.

*Question/Concern: Do you have to read with your finger all the time?* Yes, unless you want to go back to being just an average reader. Are you reading with your finger right now? Sometimes you do have the luxury to dawdle over something. Otherwise, use your hand as a pacer. The best way to learn to read faster and more efficiently is to use the techniques just introduced. Therefore, everything you read from this point on, with the possible exception of billboards as you speed down the highway, should be read with your hand as a pacer.

If you want, you can also use a pencil to pace yourself, but don't hold the pencil as if you were going to write. Rather, hold it near the eraser and pace under each line with the point of the pencil. This technique eliminates the stares you sometimes encounter when you read with your finger.

*Question/Concern: I just look at my finger when I practice.* You probably didn't realize that a good manicure was a prerequisite for this skill. Your eyes will be tempted to look at your finger in the beginning. Why shouldn't they, with a new distraction on the page? However, after conscientious practicing, your eyes will become bored with looking at your plain, but neat nail, and begin looking at all the words flying by instead.

*Question/Concern: I can't read the old way and I can't read the new way.* Chapter 2 discussed replacing old habits with new habits and the freezing, unfreezing, and refreezing process. That is what is occurring right now if you can't read the old way and you can't read the new way. It is uncomfortable because you are between skills. You are well on your way to becoming a better reader if you feel like you are in the middle; that is exactly where you are supposed to be. You old, inefficient habits are being unfrozen, and you are in a state of transition as the new habits become part of your reading skills. The best thing to do is keep on practicing diligently and rest assured that you are doing the right thing if you feel this way. Practice will refreeze your new, efficient habits.

*Question/Concern: I seem to be able to read pretty well with my "S" pattern. Is this okay?* Sure. Although technically the "S" pattern is a practice reading/previewing step, some people are very comfortable with their "S" pattern for reading. Be sure you are reading, though, and not skimming. Reading means understanding what is on the page according to your purposes. It is not recommended that all people read with the "S," but you may find that certain types of material lend themselves very well to reading with the "S."

*Question/Concern: When I practice read, the print down the middle of the page is dark and the margins are fuzzy. Is this okay?* You are doing the right thing if you see this phenomena. It means you are going fast enough to begin widening your span of focus. One of the first sensations for people when they begin expanding their constricted focus into a more relaxed and natural focus is that the middle of the page becomes darker. Keep up the good work!

*Question/Concern: Sometimes I am surprised at how much I can write.* You may be guessing, but write it down anyway. It also may be that you actually did see that information, but because the drill's speed didn't allow you to say all the words to yourself, you didn't have the reinforcement that comes with the old habit of subvocalization. Therefore, you aren't sure you saw it.

It is possible to see and then immediately know the information. You use that process every day. It is simply a new experience for you to see and immediately know in a reading situation. The best way to validate your reduction of subvocalization and your greater reliance on the see/know process is to write the words down. Go back and check the passage or use the tests in this book to reassure yourself that you don't have to say all the words to yourself to understand them.

*Question/Concern: My speeds are erratic.* Speed depends on many factors: if you had a good or bad day at work, if you like the book you are using to practice, etc. Also, the skills are not stabilized in the beginning, so the speeds will vary. A change of even 100 words per minute up or down is nothing to worry about in the beginning. With practice, your speeds will stabilize.

*Question/Concern: I think I see a lot while I am doing the exercises, but then I draw a blank when it comes to writing something down.* Two issues are at work here. First is the lack of auditory reassurance. Because you didn't say all of the words to yourself, you have no reassurance that you saw them, leaving a void in your reading process that needs to be restructured. That is how writing after reading and practice reading plays an important role in speed and comprehension development.

Second, keep in mind that comprehension means understanding the material *while* you are reading it. It is possible to have had good comprehension but poor retention. Retention is what is left after you have read. Comprehension and retention are two separate skills and are developed separately. Right now you are beginning to search for better comprehension, which means asking yourself, "Did I understand it while I was reading it, even though I can't recall the information right now?" Retention of material is discussed and developed in Chapter 6.

*Question/Concern: When do I begin to understand what I am looking at?* This depends on many things. How hard is the book you are using? Are you motivated? Have you followed the directions? Have you practiced consistently? All these factors, and probably a few variables not even associated with reading, will influence how fast the comprehension aspect of the skill comes more clearly into focus. The more you practice, the sooner your comprehension will improve. Also, the word "comprehension" will change for you as you become a more efficient reader. Comprehension is covered in depth in the following chapter. Remember, speed must come first for comprehension to improve.

## Reading Selection

When you made "laundry lists" during the exercises, you were informally testing yourself on the material. The following selection is a more formal test of speed and comprehension in order to fully chart and validate your skill's progress. It is recommended that you practice with the exercises in the chapter for approximately a week before you take this test.

Use the following 3,304-word reading selection by Ralph Nader to try out your new skills. Before you begin, however, spend approximately ten minutes warming up by using one of the exercises presented earlier in this chapter on other material.

Set your goal for reading this article at around 6½ minutes, or approximately 500 words per minute. Take the comprehension check after you complete the reading. Check your answers in the back, and record your speed and score in the course progress chart in the Appendix.

# The Stylists: It's the Curve that Counts

Ralph Nader

Today almost everyone is familiar with the work of Ralph Nader. At the time that this selection was first published, however, Nader was still relatively unknown, a writer and critic whose power was yet to be discovered. His book *Unsafe at Any Speed* (which is sometimes credited with forcing General Motors to stop production of the Chevrolet Corvair) focused public attention on the way automobiles are designed, manufactured, and marketed.

The importance of the stylist's role in automobile design is frequently obscured by critics whose principal tools are adjectives. The words are familiar: stylists build "insolent chariots," they deal with tremendous trifles to place on "Detroit Iron." Or, in the moralist's language, the work of the stylists is "decadent, wasteful, and superficial."

The stylists' work cannot be dismissed so glibly. For however transitory or trivial their visible creations may be on the scale of human values,their function has been designated by automobile company top management as *the* prerequisite for maintaining the annual high volume of automobile sales—no small assignment in an industry that has a volume of at least twenty billion dollars every year.

It is the stylists who are responsible for most of the annual model change which promises the consumer "new" automobiles. It is not surprising, therefore, to find that this "newness" is almost entirely stylistic in content and that engineering innovation is restricted to a decidedly secondary role in product development.

In the matter of vehicle safety, this restriction has two main effects. First, of the dollar amount that the manufacturer is investing in a vehicle, whatever is spent for styling cannot be spent for engineering. Thus, the costs of styling divert money that might be devoted to safety. Second, stylistic suggestions often conflict with engineering ideas, and since the industry holds the view that "seeing is selling," style gets the priority.

Styling's precedence over engineering safety is well illustrated by this statement in a General Motors engineering journal: "The choice of latching means and actuating means, or handles, is dictated by styling requirements.... Changes in body style will continue to force redesign of door locks and handles."

Another feature of style's priority over safety shows up in the paint and chrome finishes of the vehicle, which, while they provide a shiny new automobile for the dealer's floor, also create dangerous glare. Stylists can even be credited with overall concepts that result in a whole new variety of hazard. The hard-top convertible and the pillarless models, for example, were clearly the products of General Motors styling staff.

Engineering features that are crucial to the transportation function of the vehicle do exert some restraining influence on styling decisions. A car must have four tires, and though the stylists may succeed shortly in coloring them, it is unlikely that aromatic creampuffs will replace the rubber. But conflicts between style and traditional engineering features are not often resolved in the latter's favor. For example, rational design of the instrument panel does not call for yearly change or recurring variety. Yet the stylists have had their way and at the same time have met management's demands for the interchangeability of components between different car makes. In one instance the 1964 Oldsmobile used exactly the same heater control as the 1964 Buick. In one brand it was placed in a horizontal position; in the other it was used vertically. With this technique, four separate and "different" instrument panels were created for each division.

This differentiating more and more about less and less has reached staggering proportions. In 1957 the Fisher body division produced for the five General Motors car divisions more than 75 different body styles with 450 interior soft trim combinations and a huge number of exterior paint combinations. By 1963 this output proliferated to 140 body styles and 843 trim combinations.

Different designs for what General Motors styling chief Harley Earl called "dynamic obsolescence" must be created for many elements of the car: front ends, rear ends, hoods, ornaments, rear decks and rear quarter panels, tail lamps, bumper shades, rocker panels, and the latest items being offered in an outburst of infinite variation—wheel covers and lugs.

These styling features form the substance of sales promotion and advertising. the car makers' appeals are emotional; they seek to inspire excitement, aesthetic pleasure, and the association of the glistening model in its provocative setting with the prospect's most far-reaching personal visions and wish-fulfillment. This approach may seem flighty, but the industry has learned that the technique sells cars to people who have no other reason to buy them with such frequency.

In recent years, campaigns saturated with the "style sell" have moved on to bolder themes. A 1964 advertisement for the Chevrolet Chevelle said, "We didn't just make the Chevelle beautiful and hope for the best . . . . If you think all we had in mind was a good-looking car smaller than the Chevrolet and bigger than Chevy II, read on." Curved side windows, the ad continued, are not just for appearance, "they slant way in for easy entry and don't need bulky space-wasting doors to roll down into." In addition, Chevelle's "long wide hood looks nice, too," because of all that goes under it—"a wide choice of Six and V-8 engines."

A Buick advertisement listed a number of regular vehicle features and commented, "You don't really need these, but how can you resist them?" ...

General Motors has been the most aggressive advocate of styling. The first distinct styling section was organized in 1927 under Harley Earl. It was called "The Art and Colour Section." At first, the stylists' position was not secure when it came to disagreements with engineers. Earl's first contributions, slanted windshields and thin corner-pillars, had to be justified as "improving visibility." But by the late thirties Earl's group became the "General Motors styling section," and he was elevated to a vice presidency, indicating that the stylist's function was equal in importance to the work of the engineering, legal, company public relations, and manufacturing departments. The styling departments went through similar developments in other automobile companies. The engineer's authority over the design of the automobile was finished. As Charles Jordan of General Motors said, "Previously, functional improvement or cost reduction was a good reason for component redesign, but [in the thirties] the engineer had to learn to appreciate new reasons for redesigns." In a paper delivered before the Society of Automotive Engineers in 1962, Jordan demonstrated how the importance of the stylist has continued to grow when he urged that the word "styling" be replaced by the word "designer." Jorden said that the "designer" (that is, the stylist) is "the architect of the car, the coordinator of all the elements that make up the complete car, and the artist who gives it form. He stands at the beginning, his approach to and responsibility for the design of the vehicle is parallel to that of an architect of a building." An observer might wonder what was left for the engineer to do but play the part of a technical minion. Jordan ended his address by looking into the future. He foresaw changes in the automobile industry that he described as "drastic and far-reaching." He listed eleven questions in advanced research inquiry for which the styling research and the advanced vehicle design sections were working to find answers. Not one concerned collision protection....

The callousness of the stylists about the effects of their creations on pedestrians is seen clearly in the case of William Mitchell, chief stylist at General Motors and the principal creator of the Cadillac tail fin. This sharp, rising fin was first introduced in the late forties, soaring in height and prominence each year until it reached a grotesque peak in 1959 and gradually declining thereafter until it was finally eliminated in the 1966 models. To understand how a man could devise and promote such a potentially lethal protuberance, it is necessary to understand the enthusiasm of Mr. Mitchell, who frequently confides to interviewers that he has "gasoline in his blood." His vibrancy in conversation revolves around the concepts of "movement," "excitement," and "flair." Samples of his recent statements are illustrative: "When you sat behind the wheel, you looked down that long hood, and then there were two headlight shapes, and then two fender curves—why, you felt excited just sitting there. A car *should* be exciting." Or, "Cars will be more clearly masculine or feminine," and "For now we deal with aesthetics ... that indefinable, intangible quality that makes *all* the difference." Mr. Mitchell's reported view of safety is that it is the driver's responsibility to avoid accidents, and that if cars were made crashworthy, the "nuts behind the wheel" would take even greater chances.

The world of Mr. Mitchell centers around the General Motors technical center, where in surroundings of lavish extravagance he presides over a staff of more than 1,400 styling specialists. It is a world of motion, color, contour, trim, fabric. To illustrate the degree of specialization involved, one color selector holds 2,888 metal samples of colors; glass-enclosed studios, surrounding verdant roof gardens, are specially designed so that colors may be matched under varying lighting conditions. In such an environment, it is easy for Mr. Mitchell to believe that "Eighty-five per cent of all the information we receive is visual." His two favorite sayings are, "Seeing is selling," and "The shape of things shape man."

The matter of Cadillac tail fins, however, transcends the visual world of Mr. Mitchell. Fins have been felt as well as seen, and felt fatally when not seen. In ways that should have been anticipated by Mr. Mitchell, these fins have "shaped" man.

In the year of its greatest height, the Cadillac fin bore an uncanny resemblance to the tail of the stegosaurus, a dinosaur that had two sharp rearward-projecting horns on each side of the tail. In 1964, a California motorcycle driver learned the dangers of the Cadillac tail fin. The cyclist was following a heavy line of traffic on the freeway going toward Newport Harbor in Santa Ana. As the four-lane road narrowed to two lanes, the confusion of highway construction and the swerving of vehicles in the merging traffic led to the Cadillac's sudden stop. The motorcyclist was boxed in and was unable to turn aside. He hit the rear bumper of the car at a speed of about twenty miles per hour, and was hurled into the tail fin, which pierced his body below the heart and cut him all the way down to the thigh bone in a large circular gash. Both fin and man survived this encounter.

The same was not true in the case of nine-year-old Peggy Swan. On September 29, 1963, she was riding her bicycle near her home in Kensington, Maryland. Coming down Kensington Boulevard she bumped into a parked car in a typical childhood accident. But the car was a 1962 Cadillac, and she hit the tail fin, which ripped into her body below the throat. She died at Holy Cross Hospital a few hours later of thoracic hemorrhage.

Almost a year and a half earlier, Henry Wakeland, the independent automotive engineer, had sent by registered mail a formal advisory to General Motors and its chief safety engineer, Howard Gandelot. The letter was sent in the spirit of the Canons of Ethics for Engineers, and began with these words: "This letter is to insure that you as an engineer and the General Motors Corporation are advised of the hazard to pedestrians which exists in the sharp-pointed tail fins of recent production 1962 Cadillac automobiles and other recent models of Cadillacs. The ability of the sharp and pointed tail fins to cause injury when they contact a pedestrian is visually apparent." Wakeland gave details of two recent fatal cases that had come to his attention. In one instance, an old woman in New York City had been struck by a Cadillac which was rolling slowly backward after its power brakes failed. The blow of the tail fin had killed her. In the other case, a thirteen-year-old Chicago boy, trying to catch a fly ball on a summer day in 1961, had run into a 1961 Cadillac fin, which pierced his heart.

Wakeland said, "An obviously apparent hazard should not be allowed to be included in an automobile because there are only a few circumstances under which the hazard would cause accident or injury. When any large number of automobiles which carry the hazard are in use, the circumstances which translate the hazard into accident or injury will eventually arise. Since it is technically possible to add [fins to automobiles] it is also technically possible to remove them, either before or after manufacture.

Howard Gandelot replied to Wakeland, saying that only a small number of pedestrian injuries due to fins or other ornamentation had come to the attention of General Motors, adding that there "always is a likelihood of the few unusual types of accidents."

The lack of complaints is a standard defense of the automobile companies when they are asked to explain hazardous design features. Certainly no company has urged the public to make complaints about such injuries as described by Wakeland. Nor has any company tried to find out about these injuries either consistently or through a pilot study. Moreover, the truth of the statement that "very few complaints" are received by the automobile companies is a self-serving one that is not verifiable by any objective source or agency outside the companies. Also, it must be remembered that since there is no statistical reporting system on this kind of accident—whether the system is sponsored by the government or the insurance industry—there is no publicly available objective source of data concerning such accidents.

As an insider, Gandelot knew that the trend of Cadillac tail fin design was to lower the height of the fin. He included in his reply to Wakeland this "confidential information" about the forthcoming 1963 Cadillac: "The fins were lowered to bring them closer to the bumper and positioned a little farther forward so that the bumper face now affords more protection.

Gandelot's comment touches on an important practice. The introduction, promotion, and finally the "phasing out" of external hazards is purely a result of stylistic fashions. For example, a few years ago sharp and pointed horizontal hood ornaments were the fad. Recent models avoid these particular ornament designs, not for pedestrian safety but to conform to the new "clean look" that is the trademark of current styling. The deadly Cadillac tail fin has disappeared for the same reason. New styles bring new hazards or the return of old ones.

Systematic engineering design of the vehicle could minimize or prevent many pedestrian injuries. The majority of pedestrian-vehicle collisions produce injuries, not fatalities. Most of these conditions occur at impact speed of under twenty-five miles per hour, and New York City data show that in fatality cases about twenty-five per cent of the collisions occurred when the vehicles involved were moving at speeds below fourteen miles per hour. It seems quite obvious that the external design and not just the speed of the automobile contributes greatly to the severity of the injuries inflicted on the pedestrian. Yet the external design is so totally under the unfettered control of the stylist that no engineer employed by the automobile industry has ever delivered a technical paper concerning pedestrian collision. Nor have the automobile companies made any public mention of any crash testing or engineering safety research on the problem.

But two papers do exist in the technical literature, one by Henry Wakeland and the other by a group of engineers at the University of California in Los Angeles. Wakeland destroyed the lingering myth that when a pedestrian is struck by an automobile it does not make any difference which particular design feature hits him. He showed that heavy vehicles often strike people without causing fatality, and that even in fatal cases, the difference between life and death is often the difference between safe and unsafe design features. Wakeland's study was based on accident and autopsy reports of about 230 consecutive pedestrian fatalities occurring in Manhattan during 1958 and early 1959. In this sample, case after case showed the victim's body penetrated by ornaments, sharp bumper and fender edges, headlight hoods, medallions, and fins. He found that certain bumper configurations tended to force the adult pedestrian's body down, which of course greatly increased the risk of the car's running over him. Recent models, with bumpers shaped like sled runners and sloping grill work above the bumpers, which give the appearance of "leaning into the wind," increase even further the car's potential for exerting down-and-under pressures on the pedestrian.

The UCLA study, headed by Derwyn Severy, consisted of experimenting with dummies to produce force and deflection data on vehicle-pedestrian impacts. The conclusion was that "the front end geometry and resistance to deformation of a vehicle striking a pedestrian will have a major influence on the forced movement of the pedestrian following the impact." These design characteristics are considered crucial to the level of injury received, since subsequent contact with the pavement may be even more harmful than the initial impact. As additional designs for protections the Severy group recommends the use of sheet metal that collapses, greater bumper widths, and override guards to sweep away struck pedestrians from the front wheels.

If the automobile companies are seeking more complaints about the effects of styling in producing pedestrian hazards, they might well refer to a widely used textbook on preventive medicine written by Doctors Hilleboe and

Larimore. Taking note of the many tragic examples of unnecessarily dangerous design, the results of which "are seen daily in surgical wards and autopsy tables," the authors concluded that "if one were to attempt to produce a pedestrian-injuring mechanism, one of the most theoretically efficient designs which might be developed would closely approach that of the front end of some present-day automobiles."

The ultimate evidence that the work of the stylist is anything but trivial is to be found in the effect styling has had on the economic aspects of the automobile industry.

General Motors, which controls over fifty per cent of the automobile market, whenever it introduces and promotes a particular styling feature can compel the other companies to follow suit. The history of the wrap-around windshield, the tail fin, and the hard-top convertible confirms this point. For although the wrap-around windshield created visual distortion that shocked the optometry profession, and the tail fin and hard-top designs engendered the dangers discussed earlier, every one of the other automobile companies followed the lead of General Motors in order not to be out of date.

Economists call this phenomenon "protective imitation," but under any name, following suit involved tremendous tooling costs, the curtailment of engineering diversity and innovation, and most important, the wholesale adoption of features that were intended to please the eye of the driver rather than to protect his life.

George Romney, then the president of American Motors, described the situation aptly when he told the Kefauver Senate antitrust subcommittee in 1958, "It is just like a woman's hat. The automobile business has some of the elements of the millinery industry in it, in that you can make style become the hallmark of modernity ... A wrap-around windshield, through greater sums of money and greater domination of the market, can be identified as being more important than something that improves the whole automobile.... In an industry where style is a primary sales tool, public acceptance of a styling approach can be achieved by the sheer impact of product volume."

Still the industry has persisted in declaring that it merely "gives the customer what he wants." This hardly squares with Mr. Romney's statement or with the facts. The history of every successful style feature is that it was conceived in one of the automobile company style sections—often without reference to company engineers, let alone considerations of safety—and then turned over to marketing specialists for repetitive, emotional exploitation until it was an entrenched, accepted "fashion."

Entrenched, that is, until the need to make the customer dissatisfied with that fashion sent the styling staffs back to their drawing boards. The principle that governs them is in direct contradiction to the give-them-what-they-want defense. In the words of Gene Bordinat of Ford, the stylist at work must "take the lead in establishing standards of taste." That, in fact, is what they have done.

The follow-the-leader spiral of styling innovations has had other profound effects. One of the most important results is that by concentrating model "changes" in the area of styling, the manufacturers have focused consumer attention on those features of the automobile that are the most likely subject of "persuasive" rather than "informational" appeals. As in the fasion industry, dealing with emotions rather than dealing with the intellect has had the result that the car makers have rarely been threatened with consumer sovereignty over the automobile. On the contrary, car manufacturers have exerted self-determined control over the products they offer. This control is reflected in another statement from Mr. Mitchell, who said, "One thing today is that we have more cars than we have names. Maybe the public doesn't want all these kinds, but competition makes it necessary."

The narrowing of the difference between automobiles to minor styling distinctions is not the only unhealthy result of the stylists' dominance. Even more discouraging has been the concomitant drying-up of engineering ingenuity. As the stylists have steadily risen to pre-eminence, the technological imagination of automotive engineers has slowed to a point where automobile company executives themselves have deplored the lack of innovation. Ford vice president Donald Frey recognized the problem clearly when he said in an address delivered in January 1964, "I believe that the amount of product innovation successfully introduced into the automobile is smaller today than in previous times and is still falling. The automatic transmission [adopted in 1939 on a mass-production basis] was the last major innovation of the industry."

The head of Mr. Frey's company, Henry Ford II, seemed troubled by the same question in his address to the same group. He said, "When you think of the enormous progress of science over the last two generations, it's astonishing to realize that there is very little about the basic principles of today's automobile that would seem strange and unfamiliar to the pioneers of our industry. . . . What we need even more than the refinement of old ideas is the ability to develop new ideas and put them to work."

Neither of these automobile executives, of course, makes the obvious connection that if an industry devotes its best efforts and its largest investment to styling concepts, it must follow that new ideas in engineering—and safety— will be tragically slow in coming.

## NADER COMPREHENSION QUESTIONS

1. The term "new" in Nader's view of the automobile industry refers to what aspect of production?

2. The issue of the demands of improvement in _____ takes precedence over the demands of _____, according to Nader.

3. As in the 1964 Oldsmobile heater, the term new may simply mean a change in the:

_____a. color

_____b. design

_____c. function

_____d. position

4. Nader contends that the fin of the 1959 Cadillac was dangerous.

_____a. True

_____b. False

## CONCLUSION

Chapter 3 begins your reading improvement by showing you how to use your hand as a pacer on the page. Your hand quickly eliminates regressions and other inefficient eye motions. Your span of focus expands, and subvocalizations are reduced. All of these old habits that slowed your reading are directly challenged by the use of your hand, and you have noticed the effect of improving your reading habits through an increase in speed.

Your Basic Step and "S" pattern, as well as the notion of writing after reading, give your reading new efficiency and potential. The concept of practice to replace the old habits, plus the proper practice techniques as described in "Practice Session for the Week" on page 78, solidly launched you into faster and smarter reading. The next chapter will round out your reading skills by developing the comprehension aspect of your new skill. Take a few minutes before moving on to Chapter 4 and review this chapter using your "S" pattern.

**Chapter 3 Practice Session for the Week**

*NOTE:*

1. Use your hand in *all* your reading.
2. Practice at least one hour per day.
3. Commit yourself to attaining the minimum reading rate for the week: *500* words per minute.

Before beginning your drill, remember to break in the book of your choice and practice turning pages for a few minutes.

*DRILL:*

1. Practice read using the Basic Step for three minutes. Mark your stopping point. Compute your words per minute.
2. Practice read the same section using the "S" for two minutes. Be sure you make it to your mark at least once. Construct a laundry list.
3. Read the section at the rate of *at least* 500 words per minute. Compute your words per minute. Add to your laundry list.

Repeat this drill at least four times daily. Remember, your improvement is directly related to the amount of effort you make.

**ANSWERS:**

**Progress Check 1**

1. C
2. In order to not break the flow of information; hence concentration.
3. It is a physical skill.
4. Page turning

*True or False* Collegial Tone

1. T
2. F
3. T
4. F
5. F

## Progress Check 2

1. A,C,D,F
2. You must begin with the physical aspect of the skill.
3. Understanding
4. a) going as fast as you can
   b) getting as much as you can

## Progress Check 3

1. B
2. A
3. B
4. C
5. going, getting

## What Type of Book Are You Reading?

A. Garden book, chapter on the cultivation of trees.
B. Economics book, stock market crash of 1929.
C. Education book, chapter on instructional objectives.
D. Journalism, chapter on the historical perspective of newspapers and television.

**ANSWERS: Nader's Article**

1. New equals new styling, not new engineering.
2. D
3. T
4. No one complains.
5. Every one else following suit in order to keep up.

# ONE WEEK'S PRACTICE RECORD

FROM _____ TO _____
    date                date

| | | | |
|---|---|---|---|
| **1st Session** | Highest PR:_____wpm | Highest R:_____wpm | Name of Book:_____ |
| total # of mins._____ | Lowest PR:_____wpm | Lowest R:_____wpm | Comments: |
| **2nd Session** | Highest PR:_____wpm | Highest R:_____wpm | Name of Book:_____ |
| total # of mins._____ | Lowest PR:_____wpm | Lowest R:_____wpm | Comments: |
| **3rd Session** | Highest PR:_____wpm | Highest R:_____wpm | Name of Book:_____ |
| total # of mins._____ | Lowest PR:_____wpm | Lowest R:_____wpm | Comments: |
| **4th Session** | Highest PR:_____wpm | Highest R:_____wpm | Name of Book:_____ |
| total # of mins._____ | Lowest PR:_____wpm | Lowest R:_____wpm | Comments: |
| **5th Session** | Highest PR:_____wpm | Highest R:_____wpm | Name of Book:_____ |
| total # of mins._____ | Lowest PR:_____wpm | Lowest R:_____wpm | Comments: |
| **6th Session** | Highest PR:_____wpm | Highest R:_____wpm | Name of Book:_____ |
| total # of mins._____ | Lowest PR:_____wpm | Lowest R:_____wpm | Comments: |
| **7th Session** | Highest PR:_____wpm | Highest R:_____wpm | Name of Book:_____ |
| total # of mins._____ | Lowest PR:_____wpm | Lowest R:_____wpm | Comments: |
| **8th Session** | Highest PR:_____wpm | Highest R:_____wpm | Name of Book:_____ |
| total # of mins._____ | Lowest PR:_____wpm | Lowest R:_____wpm | Comments: |

S U M M A R Y

| | | |
|---|---|---|
| **TOTAL TIME** | Highest PR:_____wpm | Highest Read:_____ |
| | Lowest PR:_____wpm | Lowest Read:_____ |
| | Comments: | |

# 4 ——————— Comprehension: Improving Your Understanding

It is assumed that you have been practicing the exercises in Chapter 3 for at least one week, for approximately an hour a day, before you begin this chapter. As mentioned previously, speed should come first, since comprehension skills are supported by good speed.

This chapter lays the foundation for comprehension improvement by addressing how you acquire information at higher rates of speed. It requires supplanting old, inefficient habits of understanding with new, more efficient habits.

The following is a description of the speeds and techniques you have at your disposal.

*Study Reading:* 0-200 wpm. In study reading, you may be reading, rereading, taking notes, or analyzing the material. Reserve this speed and technique for the most difficult types of material you encounter. The wider range of speed that you are acquiring will make this slowest of speeds less necessary than previously for understanding this type of information.

*Slow Reading:* 150-250 wpm. Efficient readers use this speed at times for fairly difficult or unfamiliar material. Rather than use this range exclusively, as you did with your old speed habits, this speed range should be avoided while you learn to expand your speed range.

*Rapid Reading:* 400-800 wpm. This speed will probably suit most of your professional daily reading needs.

*Skimming, Scanning:* 500-? These processes may be used with great success, but they are not reading in the strictest sense; rather, they are information gathering techniques.

Scanning is looking rapidly through material for a particular point or piece of information. Once you discover the point, however, you should stop scanning and read or preview the information. In order to be an effective scanner, you must know what you are looking for—have a definite purpose. Scanning, then, is as much a sifting process as an information gathering process.

Skimming is looking through the material to give all of it your equal attention as you search for the main or general ideas. Skimming is called previewing in this book; however, previewing is a much more intellectual, rigorous activity than is usually associated with skimming.

Be aware, however, that simply reading this chapter will not help you comprehend better. Only with consistent, conscientious practice will you make the skills presented your own, to apply to whatever reading materials you wish.

Comprehension, understanding the information on the page, can be shown through some outward display of this information after the reading is completed. Any number of performances can show that you comprehended a particular piece of information. Performance can range from a simple repetition of the major points to an in-depth, critical evaluation of the material.

Not only are the ranges of comprehension wide, but so too are the factors affecting your comprehension. Some of these factors are within your control: some are not. The quality of your perception and the speed of your reading affects your comprehension. Motivation, concentration, and a well-defined purpose for reading also affects your comprehension. Your ability to retain and recall information, your vocabulary, the general background you bring into the reading situation, and the nature of the material all influence your comprehension. Therefore, *the most effective way to improve your comprehension is to work at improving all the preceding factors.*

## EARLY READING EDUCATION

During your elementary school years, you probably learned to read using story books. Although certainly not deathless prose, they served their function as your introduction to reading and books. Somewhere between the third and fifth grade, the teacher handed you another type of book, a non-fiction book, perhaps social studies, geography, or some other form of introductory reading. The problem was that you were handed the new book, but probably were not handed a new method with which to read it. So your natural reaction to the non-fiction book was to read it the same way you read your previous fiction books. That meant you opened the book to the first page, looked at the first word, and began to read, expecting a story to unfold. Since those first non-fiction books were usually history or social studies, they still fit into the story book mold. Therefore, it was natural to use story reading skills, and they worked at least as successfully as before. Both teacher and pupil were satisfied that this was the proper way to read a non-fiction book.

The techniques you acquired in elementary school are still largely responsible for getting you through your professional reading requirements today. You may have acquired a few embellishments or picked up some isolated tips on surviving college reading demands, but for the most part, you still read non-fiction as you read fiction in the third grade. Your reading education stopped too soon.

## NON-FICTION VS. FICTION

The nature of fiction is, of course, totally different from non-fiction or technical material. The information is presented differently and your level of responsibility is usually much higher. First, the information in technical material is much more structured than in fiction. The movement from concepts, to supportive data, to details is much more systematic. Technical material generally has more information per page. And you, as the reader of technical material, are placed in a position of greater responsibility because, when you finish the material, you must usually do something with the information.

Since you have recognized a significant difference between fiction, non-fiction, and technical material; and since you know you must use reading techniques particular to your technical reading requirements, you must determine an effective, specialized method to deal with your technical reading requirements. We call those specialized methods for reading "technical material study systems."

### Progress Check 1

1. How can you assure yourself that you have comprehended something after you have read it?
2. List three factors that affect your quality of comprehension. (Six were listed.)
3. How are fiction and non-fiction materials different?

Fiction is:

Non-fiction is:

## DIVIDE AND CONQUER, UNITE AND RULE

These are the six steps to better study:

1. Set your purpose
2. Survey
3. Preview
4. Read
5. Reread/recheck
6. VDI (Visual Display of Information)

The phrase that best describes the study system you are about to learn is "Divide and Conquer/Unite and Rule." The first important word here is "system." If you are to read technical material with efficiency, you need an organized procedure, a system to apply to *any* type of material you must read.

*Divide.* Proper "division" of the material is critical to maintaining concentration and motivation. Haphazard division of material tends to delay learning and may even be detrimental to it. Intelligent, efficient division for study and learning requires sensitivity to the organization of the entire piece of information, clear understanding of your purpose for reading, and realistic goals.

*Conquer.* "Conquer" means to read all concepts, ideas, facts, and details with careful and deliberate consideration, and to note emphasis, relationships, and importance to prior knowledge. This is the input or true learning state of the system.

*Unite.* "Unite" means to reconstruct the information according to your purposes and future needs. Division of the information and study reading (conquer) necessitate a concentrated focus on small bits of information. This fragmenting of the total piece of information is not, however, the final step to learning, even though most readers stop at this point. Uniting the material back into the whole pattern of information prepares you to retain and recall the information accurately.

*Rule.* "Rule" implies that you now have an excellent working knowledge of the information; it has become yours to use as you see fit. The permanent record you have created in your notes is now more important than the original text.

## ANTICIPATE AND SELECT VS. THE SPONGE METHOD

An aspect critical to understanding "Divide and Conquer/Unite and Rule" is that the system does not encourage wholesale absorbtion of written material. It would be impractical and, for the most part, impossible for you to learn/ remember everything you read. Rather, the system allows you to cultivate an effective process to both anticipate and select.

Anticipation is the one objective of all five steps in the study system. Setting your purpose, surveying, and previewing require you to think about the material *before* reading it. It allows you to sensitize yourself to the information and encourages you to get ready to read it.

Selection is another objective throughout the study system. First, by identifying distinguishing features of a selected work and second, by discriminating and selecting among the particular passages or pages that, in terms of their aptness or special value, merit study reading, you have saved yourself time and effort; that is what this book is about.

**Progress Check 2**

1. Why do you need a system to read and study material?

2. Why the word "divide?" What skills do proper division imply?

3. What does "conquer" indicate you have done with the material?

4. Why "unite" the material?

5. Identify which of the following is "anticipation" and which is "selection," as discussed in the text:

   To identify the distinguishing features and discriminate between particular features that merit further study is known as _____.

   To sensitize yourself to material in order to mentally prepare yourself to read it is called _____.

6. How do the anticipation and selection of material apply to the steps in the study procedure?

## SET PURPOSE

Most readers do not determine their purpose for reading well enough (some not at all). Most readers are unable to pose questions to help them crystalize their purpose for reading. This is reasonable behavior, because most readers were never required in school to assess the purpose of reading, other than that the teacher directed them to do so, or they were reading to pass a test. Neither teacher direction nor passing a test incorporate much preparation for later practical use. In your professional reading, that old method of purpose setting is inadequate; you will probably use this material in an important and meaningful way on the job.

Following are some questions to help you assess your purpose in reading. Before reading anything, briefly jot down answers to the following questions until you are familiar with all the possibilities in assessing purpose.

## ASSESSMENT OF PURPOSE

### The Physical Description of the Material

1. *Where did this material come from* (a brochure, chapter in a book, report, memo, newspaper, magazine, etc.)? Check carefully, as many selections you read were initially published in another format. You can learn a great deal about the nature (credibility, recentness) of the material if you know the origin.

2. *How long is the selection?* Many people start to read and study a selection without first considering its length. They soon run out of steam because they did not pace their reading and study efforts according to the material's length. Estimate the number of words. You will get better and better at approximating as your progress.

3. *How does this selection relate to your work, hobby, or interests?* Is this material pertinent? You may be making a premature decision, but you should decide just the same. Although you may not have a definite answer right away, it will start you thinking about the relevancy of the material.

### Standard Purposes for Reading the Material

1. *What motivated you to pick this particular selection?* Was the motivation external or internal? How will this affect your reading and learning? If you were internally motivated, what features appealed to you? What features did not?

2. *What type of information do you want from this material?* Do you need to understand the main points only, or all the facts and details as well as the main points? Are you looking for new information only?

3. *Is the new information going to be put to some particular use?* Are you going to solve a problem at work? Will it add to background information on a subject? Will you have to demonstrate this information to someone else?

### Anticipation of the Material

1. *What do you think you are going to learn from this selection?*

2. *How useful do you think this particular selection will be in satisfying your purpose?*

3. *Do you think the information will be easy or difficult for you to understand? Interesting or dull? Entertaining or serious?*

### After You Have Read the Material

1. *Were your expectations justified?*

2. *Did you satisfy your purpose for reading the selection?*

3. *Did you save time or increase comprehension of the material by filling out this form before you read the material?*

4. *If you could read that selection again for the first time, what would you do differently, if anything?*

## PAY-OFFS OF SETTING A PURPOSE

The key to efficient reading is to expend just the right amount of time and effort required to suit your purpose. When you invest the few minutes it takes to contemplate your purpose for reading a selection, you have spent your time wisely. Failure to determine your purpose or having inadequate determination encourages you to treat all types of material in the same way. This is illogical given the vast differences in the difficulty levels of your everyday reading.

Efficient readers recognize these differences and adjust their purposes accordingly.

As you expand your speeds and your comprehension capabilities, you will increase your options for what to do with that stack of unread journals and reports on your desk. However, just because you have a good repertoire of techniques, this does not insure efficiency. How and when to apply the techniques are the results of clearly determining your purpose. As you change your purpose, as you adjust your pre- and post-reading expectations and reasons for reading each different selection, you will adjust your technique accordingly. This close and important relationship between technique and purpose makes the difference between an efficient reader and someone who merely has a bag of tricks.

**Progress Check 3**

1. The best way to determine purpose for reading is to:

      \_\_\_\_\_a. look at the table of contents

      \_\_\_\_\_b. ask yourself the proper questions

      \_\_\_\_\_c. just start reading and allow the purpose to be revealed

      \_\_\_\_\_d. ask a friend

2. Which questions should you ask yourself?

      \_\_\_\_\_a. How is the information physically organized?

      \_\_\_\_\_b. What motivated you to read this information?

      \_\_\_\_\_c. What do you anticipate you will get out of this information?

      \_\_\_\_\_d. What did you get out of the information after you read it?

3. What happens to your reading and studying if your purpose is not clearly defined?

4. What will you change as your purpose changes?

_____a. your techniques

_____b. your speed of reading

## SURVEY
## (REDEFINE PURPOSE/SET GOALS)

The purpose of the survey is to give you an overview of the material. When you survey an article, a chapter, or an entire book, you begin by looking at material other than the printed text. This includes the title page, copyright, table of contents, (look here to find the obvious, implied, or potential relationships among these items, which outline the main ideas of the book) forward, preface, and any other matter before the material. Next, look over the information at the end of the selection, including bibliography, index, appendices, conclusions, suggested readings, or what other information is at the end of the selection.

If you are planning to study in a textbook or long technical report, you will also want to survey the specific chapters. Again, note other printed textual information, including chapter introductions (read them), synopses, pictures, charts, graphs, diagrams, tables (all such information can be called visual aids). Also look at anything at the end of the chapter such as summaries (read them) and questions (definitely read them because questions tell you, in no uncertain terms, exactly what is important to the author).

If you are proceding through a book for a class or plan to study a book chapter by chapter, survey in the following sequence: the chapter before your assigned chapter, the chapter you plan to study, and the following chapter. For example, if your target is Chapter 8, survey Chapters 7, 8 and 9. This helps in a number of ways. First, it allows you to quickly review the last chapter, it helps you to mentally prepare for the chapter you are about to study, and helps you to anticipate the subsequent chapter. It will, therefore, allow you to see more clearly the overall information in the book.

### PAY-OFFS TO A GOOD SURVEY

Surveying is a good investment in time and effort. First, surveying taps the human desire to complete things. Th__ D__ la__at__on of I__d__pen__en__e can be comprehended because the brain is eager to understand and performs closure, or the completion of information, to understand. You can use this same striving of your brain to make yourself begin thinking about the material. Your anticipation of just how the selection will fit together is whetted by doing a survey. Likewise, the survey allows you to "see the whole." The overall perspective is how the author wanted you to understand the selection, which means perceiving the general ideas and how they fit together before you address the isolated facts and details.

### Survey Can Reduce Fear

A survey can also help reduce fear. If you feel intimidated or overwhelmed, this will influence your study effectiveness. By moving quickly and efficiently through a survey, you may find that the material is within your grasp of understanding *or* that you may have to make arrangements for more study time. This can make studying a more pleasant experience.

A survey will also let you make comparisons between the printed information and your previously stored knowledge. Is the information an entirely new field for you? Will it require you to master a new set of terms? Can you draw upon your past reading or experiences to more fully understand what is in front of you? Noting present knowledge allows you to make wise decisions about setting purposes and goals, and this can reduce your anxiety about the study session.

### Surveying Will Refine Your Purpose and Goals

Remember that the goals you set should always be open to adjustment as you become more familiar with the information. Your goals should be determined in terms of the amount of time you plan to spend on the material *or* the words per minute at which you plan to read it. Be specific and hold yourself to your goals or they will become part of an empty exercise. One good guideline for setting time goals is that a 50-minute study-hour is the most effective way to design your study sessions. This means that you study for 50 minutes and then break for 10 minutes. No matter where you are in your studying, you need to physically and mentally break away from the material.

Sometimes you may want to continue after the 50 minutes because you have become enthusiastic about some particular part of your reading, but break anyway. You will come back to the session physically refreshed and even more eager to continue. Those of you who find that reading/studying is not the biggest thrill in your life will find the 50-minute hour quite manageable in getting through the material.

### Progress Check 4

1. A survey gives you a(n) _____ of the structure and difficulty of the material.

2. When you survey, look at the:

_____a. bold-faced headings.

_____b. floor.

_____c. pictures, graphs, diagrams, charts.

_____d. main text.

3. Why does surveying save you time?



4. How can a good survey reduce fear?



5. How can a good survey help you to set proper goals?



6. It is recommended that you study for _____ minutes, and break for _____ minutes.

7. Study goals can be in terms of:

_____a. speed of reading.

_____b. time spent on the material.

## PREVIEW: THE KEYSTONE
## TO BETTER COMPREHENSION

The next step in the study procedure is to preview your material. Previewing means moving through the material at approximately three to five times your reading rate, to gather the main ideas presented. Previewing may also be the last step you perform on the material, according to your purpose.

Your task, as you preview the material, is to identify the general areas of information presented. Also look for the main concepts, ideas, and key words. Key words usually point out relationship, time, cause, reason, condition, or degree. For example, relationship words could be "as a result," "moreover," "in addition." Degree words could be "never," "always," "extremely." Also, key words can point out a change in the author's direction or scope, with such words as "in conclusion," "on the other hand," "for example." All these keys dictate how much concentration, time, and effort are required to master the information.

As you preview, you may also discover that only certain sections require a second, more careful study reading. Therefore, the second task as you preview is to identify those special areas meriting further consideration.

## PAY-OFFS OF PREVIEWING

Previewing is the most crucial step in the study procedure because it is the most intellectually demanding step in the entire process. The thinking and evaluating that goes into a preview is the keystone to better comprehension and to a more efficient study reading of the material. Therefore, the potential results are well worth the time invested.

Previewing sensitizes your mind to receive and organize the information, and shows you the big picture. Previewing prepares you for priority focusing on the critical information while eliminating the useless information. Previewing allows you to evaluate material in terms of the following: How much reading time? What information is to be gained? How much information is essential? What level of comprehension is required, and hence, what techniques are to be used to study? These questions should be answered in a preview and used to further clarify your purpose and goals. *Or,* you can take the time to read the entire article to answer the above questions and then plan to read it again for good comprehension. However, it is extremely difficult to read for good comprehension and answer these questions at the same time. The processes of selection and anticipation then, in the form of a preview, help you to be a better reader.

Moreover, previewing provides another important ingredient to your study technique: it helps you maintain a good reading speed throughout the study process.

## HOW TO PREVIEW

As you move through the material at three to five times your reading speed (the "S" pattern is exceptionally helpful), your attention is naturally drawn to the bold-faced headings. These headings can help you understand the development and organization of the ideas. But keep in mind that many authors do not have anything to do with deciding where those headings will be placed. Thus, you need to carefully examine the paragraphs under the headings to see if you can associate the paragraphs under the headings.

If you can't grasp the main ideas by previewing the material in the above manner, then read the first and last paragraphs of the chapter or article and use your "S" pattern for the rest of the paragraphs. If the material is exceptionally difficult, preview by reading the first and last sentence of each paragraph, as well as looking through the rest of the paragraph with your "S" pattern. Save this last type of previewing for your most difficult reading. Most of your reading requirements will be satisfied with the first type of previewing: moving through the material with your "S" pattern at three to five times your study reading rate.

The last task in your previewing is to begin a set of notes. Even if you don't plan to use the notes later, incorporating some sort of writing into your technical reading procedure greatly enhances your comprehension. First, you become more personally involved with the information because you have to write something down. Second, you evaluate what is important enough to write down and what is not, thereby increasing your occupation with the material. Finally, the way you design your notes helps you read and comprehend, retain and concentrate more effectively. The method recommended is to set up your notes in a question format.

### Why Questions?

Questions invite answers! If you have ever had a ridiculous trivia question keep you up at night, so much so that you phoned a friend in Dubuque to get the answer, then you know first hand the very human need to have questions answered. By reading to answer questions, you use that human need to understand. As an efficient reader, you must learn to ask the right questions. Asking the right question excludes superfluous information with ease. The best way to pose a question is to turn the bold-faced headings in the article or chapter into questions. For example, notes for this chapter would look like the figure on page 94.

Notice that each page of notes contains only one or two question headings and leaves a wide margin at the left. This provides you with the correct beginning of your reading/study notes. These notes and all other forms of written information are called *visual display of information* (VDI). Set your prestructured VDI aside until later.

### Progress Check 5

1. At approximately what speed is a preview done?
2. Which hand motion is good for a preview?
3. What are you looking for when you preview?
4. Discovering the pattern of information by previewing allows you to:

_____a. become sensitized to receive and organize information.

_____b. focus on important information.

| Key Words | What is Comp. & How Can I Improve It? |
|---|---|
| | What Speeds & Techniques Are Available to Use? |

| Key Words | How Did My Early Reading Education Affect My Comp.? |
|---|---|
| | What's the Difference Between Fiction & Non-Fiction? |

| Key Words | What Are the Six Steps to Better Comp.? |
|---|---|
| | 1          2          3 |

| Key Words | |
|---|---|
| | 4          5          6 |

_____c. Eliminate useless information.

_____d. keep your speed up.

_____e. begin a good set of notes.

_____f. all of the above.

_____g. none of the above.

5. Why should you set up your notes into a question format?

## STUDY READING

Once the preview is completed, you should begin study reading. The study reading phase should be done with the Basic Step. Your reading speed should be fast enough to keep the information flow from bogging down and thus forcing you to lose concentration; however, it should be slow enough to satisfy your purposes for reading.

Study reading is deliberate, careful consideration of all relevant ideas, facts, and details according to your purposes. The questions you posed in your VDI are now the first consideration when you study read. *Read to answer those questions.* As you find the answers, put the words from the page into your own words, indicating (according to your purposes) that you are grasping the information. You may take notes while you read very difficult material, or you may read an entire section and then write. Refer back to main ideas you identified in your previewing to establish a relationship between the main ideas and the facts and details you are now reading. Also, pay attention to the "how and why" of the relationship between the various facts and details.

When you read have a pencil in hand, ready to indicate important passages, words, or phrases with a check mark in the margin. You can effectively pace yourself and mark in a book if you use a pencil.

### Highlighting/Underlining vs. Marking

Many people feel the urge to highlight and/or underline as they read. There are several reasons why underlining and highlighting are traps. Some people go through and use green highlighter to identify what they think are the most important points. A problem arises in that, after they have finished the chapter or selection, they have usually highlighted too much because they were in no position to evaluate what was important or not important until they had read the entire piece. You can't identify what is important in the context of the whole until you have read the whole. The temptation, then, is to go back and rehighlight the "really" important portions with another color. For final review, the temptation is to use still another color to identify points to be studied or stressed. This can go on *ad nauseum* until a person winds up with a very expensive coloring book.

Another trap is that underlining leaves the information in the book, actually postponing learning. The reader is under an illusion that can lead to late-night cramming, or worse, little or nothing to say at the staff meeting. Unless you get into the coloring book situation, underlining usually gives all that was underlined equal importance, which is not the case when you read technical information. You tend to see only those areas of highlight or underlining that can pull small pieces of information out of context for you.

**Read with a Pencil**

We recommend that you mark your material in the following manner. During the initial study reading, use a check mark ($\sqrt{}$) beside any portion of the material you believe to be significant. When you study read and check in the margins with a pencil, you bypass the typical traps of highlighting and you review more than the isolated lines out of context. Sometimes it is necessary to use more than check marks, especially if you have a question about a particular point. It is then sometimes helpful to develop a simple system of symbols.

Here is a marking system for the margin of your materal:

| | |
|---|---|
| * | summary |
| v | important new vocabulary |
| ? | do not understand |
| x | disagree |
| # | quotation |

Keep it simple, or you will defeat your purpose because later on you will have to decipher your symbol system as well as the material. Also, since you are checking only areas, it is very difficult to fool yourself into thinking you have learned the material as you could have with underlining or highlighting.

Reading with your pencil is a definite aid to reading and studying, provided it is done correctly. Rather than the inefficient activity of underlining or highlighting, you now have an efficient evaluative tool to aid you in understanding the important passages or points in your material.

**Progress Check 6**

1. How fast should you study read?

2. How do you incorporate the questions you have formulated in your notes into study reading?

3. Why should you avoid highlighting or use underlining?

4. What should your marking system use?

## REREAD/RECHECK

Another active aspect of reading and studying comes into play after you finish your initial study reading. Now go back to the beginning of the selection and quickly reread the entire selection. This second quick rereading will synthesize the material you have divided with your study reading.

Reread at approximately twice your reading and study speed *until* you encounter a check mark or other symbol. At this point, determine, in the context of the whole, the relative importance of the mark. Carefully reread the checked areas and make the following decisions: Is the checked area important enough to merit more than one check mark or some other symbol to stress its importance? If so, mark it accordingly. Continue through the material, rereading and rechecking until you have completed the entire selection. This step helps unite the material into a complete picture. It also helps verify the information you learned and sets up reinforcement of information to guard against immediate forgetting.

## VISUAL DISPLAY OF INFORMATION—VDI

Just as you should read with a pencil, so also should you take notes during your reading and study sessions. Even if you are not in school and facing final examinations, taking notes while reading benefits your comprehension and retention. Notetaking places you in a position of responsibility toward whatever you read. You must make an immediate response to the printed text in your interpretation of the information and presentation on another page. Further, notes can identify any gaps that may occur while you are studying the material. The particular style of notes shown here also has the added advantage of being very flexible. You can create in graphic presentation the pattern of the information as it is revealed to you while you are reading.

## WHY A VDI?

The VDI has four activities that require you to view the material from a different perspective each time.

*Reduce/Rephrase.* Always put the information into your own words if possible. Keep the information succinct, and use abbreviations whenever possible. (See list for possible abbreviations.) Reducing the information to the most important points according to your purposes also guards against the temptation of trying to rewrite the entire selection. If you find your notes are longer than the initial reading, beware. This indicates your comprehension of the material was poor or you are uncomfortable with the material. Most people who go through a very difficult selection are tempted to put everything down because they don't understand anything. If this is the case for you, stop and reconsider your goals and purposes, recheck the list of factors affecting comprehension on page 83, or readjust your speed and/or techniques.

## Examples of Technical Symbols

| | | | |
|---|---|---|---|
| + | plus, positive, and | | |
| − | minus, negative | ↕ | vibration, motion |
| × | algebraic x, or multiplied by | log | common logarithm |
| ÷ | divided by | ln | natural logarithm |
| ≠ | does not equal | $e$ | base of natural logarithms |
| ≈ | equals, approximately, approximates | $\pi$ | pi |
| > | greater than, greatly, increased, increasing | ∠ | angle |
| | | ⊥ | perpendicular to |
| < | less than, reduced, decreasing | ‖ | parallel to |
| ∿ | sine curve, cosine curve | $a°$ | $a$ degrees (angle) |
| → | approaches as a limit, approaches | $a'$ | $a$ minutes (angle) |
| ≧ | greater than or equal to | $a''$ | $a$ seconds (angle) |
| ≦ | less than or equal to | ∫ | integral, integral of integration |
| ≡ | identical to | $f$ | frequency |
| ∝ | varies directly as | $f_n$ | natural frequency |
| ∴ | therefore | cps | cycles per second |
| ( )½ | square root | $m$ | mass |
| ( )$^n$ | nth root | Φ | phase |
| vs | versus against | $F$ | force |
| ⚏ | ground | / | ratio, the ratio of |
| ↔ | varied, variation | ▥ | base, support, mount, foundation |
| | area | ⌠ | curve, curvilinear |

## Typical Technical Abbreviations

| | | | |
|---|---|---|---|
| anlys | analysis | dmnsls | dimensionless |
| ampltd | amplitude | dfln | deflection |
| cald | called | dfnd | defined |
| cnst | constant | dstrbg | disturbing |
| dmpg | damping | eftvns | effectiveness |

| | | | | |
|---|---|---|---|---|
| frdm | freedom | | stfns | stiffness |
| frcg | forcing | | systm | system |
| gvs | gives | | sgnft | significant |
| hrmc | harmonic | | ths | this |
| isltr | isolator | | trnsmsblty | transmissibility |
| isltn | isolation | | thrtly | theoretically |
| pltg | plotting | | valu | value |
| reman | remain | | wth | with |
| rltnshp | relationship | | whn | when |
| smpl | simple | | xprsd | expressed |
| smpfd | simplified | | | |

Other symbols and abbreviations, for many different technical and nontechnical fields, are often found in special sections in unabridged dictionaries. Look them up the next time you are in the library.

## The-Easiest-to-Learn—Quick-Writing System

1. Symbols. Symbols are expecially helpful to students in engineering and mathematics.
   - $\neq$ does not equal
   - $\underline{f}$ = frequency

2. Create a family of symbols.
   - $\bigcirc$ = organism
   - $\circledcirc$ = individual
   - $\circledS$ = individuals

3. Leave out the periods in standard abbreviations.
   - cf = confer (Latin, compare)
   - eg = exempli gratia (Latin, for example)
   - dept = department
   - NYC = New York City

4. Use only the first syllable of a word.
   - pol = politics
   - dem = democracy
   - lib = liberal
   - cap = capitalism

5. Use the entire first syllable and only the first letter of the second syllable.

   - subj = subject
   - cons = conservative
   - tot = totalitarianism
   - ind = individual

6. Eliminate final letters. Use just enough of the beginning of a word to form easily recognizable unit.
   - assoc = associate, associated
   - ach = achievement
   - biol = biological
   - info = information
   - intro = introduction
   - chem = chemistry
   - conc = concentration
   - max = maximum
   - rep = repetition

7. Use an apostrophe.
   - gov't = government
   - am't = amount
   - con't = continued
   - educat'l = educational

8. Form the plural of the symbol word or abbreviated word by adding "s."

□ s      = areas
chaps  = chapters
co-ops = cooperatives
fs       = frequencies
/s       = ratios

9. Use "g" to represent "ing" endings.
   decrg = decreasing
   ckg   = checking
   estg  = establishing
   exptg = experimenting

10. Use a dot to represent rate. A dot placed over a symbol or a word indicates the word "rate."
    $\updownarrow$ = vibration rate
    $\underline{f}$ = frequency rate

11. Short words should generally be spelled out. Symbols, signs, or abbreviations for short words will make the notes too dense with "shorthand."
    in       but
    at       for
    to       key

12. Leave out unimportant verbs.
    went    came    be

13. Leave out "a" and "the."

14. Omit vowels from the middle of words, and retain only enough consonants to provide a recognizable skeleton of the word.
    bkgd  = background
    ppd   = prepared
    prblm = problem
    estmt = estimate
    gvt   = government

15. If a term, phrase, or name is initially written out in full during the lecture, initials can be substituted whenever the term, phrase, or name is used again.
    Initial writing: ... and the effect of the Modern Massachusetts party will be felt.
    Subsequently: MMP

16. Use symbols for commonly recurring connective or transitional words.
    &    = and
    w/   = with
    w/o  = without
    vs   = against
    ∴   = therefore

You still have that large margin down the left-hand side of your page to use. *After* you feel your reading notes are complete, perhaps after a lecture or meeting, take a few minutes and use that margin to insure that you remember the information and to test yourself on its key points.

---

Advantages

1. Master info.

2. Efficient

3. Promotes learning process.

Three Advantages:

1. *Method for mastering information*—not just recording passages.
2. *Keynote = efficiency*—no retyping/rewriting.
3. *Each step prepares way for next part of learning process.*

Record Notes
1. Use VDI.
2. Vary patterns.

3. Get main ideas.

4. Use abbrev. & frag.

Reduce Notes
1. Correct incomplete items.

2. Underline on circle.

3. Write recall cues.

Study Notes
1. Recite/verify

2. Reflect on organization
  –cues = organization
  –insights follow
  –key to memory

3. Review

Summary
1. Record
2. *Reduce*

3. Recite/verify

4. Reflect

5. Review

During class record notes.
1. *Use patterns*.
2. *Don't force VDI system*—allow information to dictate which pattern.
3. *Strive to get main ideas down*—facts, details, examples important but they're meaningful only with concepts.
4. *Use abbreviations and fragments* for extra writing and listening time.

After class reduce notes:
1. *Check/correct incomplete items*.
  –loose dates, terms, names (recorded w/o clarification).
  –notes that are too brief for recall months later.
2. Read notes and *underline/circle key words and phrases*.
3. Read underlined/circled words and *write in recall cues in the left-hand column* (key words and very brief phrases that will trigger ideas/facts on the right).

Study Notes three ways.
1. Cover up right side of page. *Read cues. Recite* ideas/facts as fully as possible. Uncover sheet and *verify recall* frequently. (Single, most powerful learning tool.)
2. *Reflect on organization of all VDI's*. Overlap notes and *read only recall cues*. Study progression of information. This will stimulate categories, relationships, inferences, personal opinions/experiences. Record all of these *insights*.
3. *Review by reciting/verifying, reflecting and reading insights*.

The system in brief:
1. *Record* lectures in the main column.
2. *Reduce* lectures with corrections, underlining and recall cues.
3. *Recite* by covering main column and expanding on recall cues. Then *verify*.
4. *Reflect* on organization by studying all cues.
5. *Review* by repeating recite/verify and reflect steps.

*Review.* This means reviewing your notes by underlining the key points, phrases, or words in each VDI. There may be one or several, but your job is to identify and underline them. After you have finished underlining them, copy them into the left-hand margin. You now have a very good representation of the conceptual organization of the material in the left-hand margin. This activity may also reveal some flaws in your note-taking technique if you can't find any main ideas or key phrases. If none are apparent, deduce from the information on the right-hand side exactly what those key points were, or you will have only a conglomeration of information with no apparent interrelationships.

When it is time to review, cover up the left-hand side of your notes and test yourself on how the main ideas are interrelated by looking at the supportive data in the main text. Conversely, you can cover up the right-hand side and look at the key points to see if you can remember the supportive data.

Another use for that left-hand margin is to leave it open and make your lecture notes in that margin. This is an especially interesting technique if you have read the assigned reading and want to compare how much or how little the instructor/lecturer deviates from the text. See pages 100 and 101 for examples.

*Reorganizing.* You may find as you gain a fuller understanding of the information that your VDI may need some revision in terms of structure and therefore emphasis. Also, after finishing the entire selection, you may want to make a master VDI of only the major points to have a visual representation of those points on one piece of paper. See the Master VDI of the study procedure at the end of the chapter. Reorganization of your notes makes the information yours in a most personal way. You are interpreting the information, which is an excellent method to integrate the information into your working storehouse of knowledge and to insure that you will retain the information for later use.

The form of the VDI can be changed according to the type and amount of information you are studying. In fact, you should change the form of the VDI so that, in later review sessions, a quick glance at the type of VDI will give you an excellent tool for association with other pieces of information.

The basic VDI pattern below is called "the dog bone" and consists of a straight line with the main point or idea on the horizontal line. The other lines are for the supportive data, the subpoints under the main point. Use as many or as few lines as necessary, according to how the information develops. What is most important is that you are in a decision-making position again as to where the next line will go. This is, in fact, a decision as to how the major and minor points are related.

Classical outlining is one way of taking notes, but outlining is usually too

confining a process of note taking. Most people become preoccupied with the form of outlining rather than the information unfolding for them as they read. The beauty of the "dog bone" is that it can accommodate any type of information you encounter, from highly structured technical material, to very informal material.

Following are some other options for a VDI, according to the type of information you are using. The structure of the VDI can be as varied as the types of information it describes. You are encouraged to create your own patterns with your particular materials.

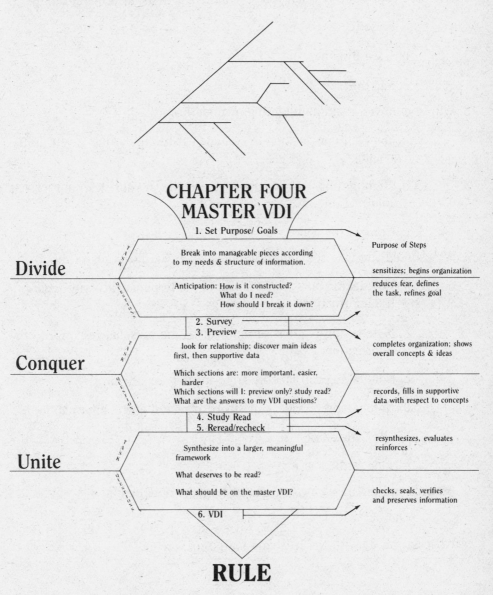

**Progress Check 7**

1. Rereading is for:

    \_\_\_\_a. fun.

    \_\_\_\_b. synthesis of information.

    \_\_\_\_c. checking to see if you learned anything.

2. What are your options when you reach a check mark in your rereading?

    \_\_\_\_a. erase it.

    \_\_\_\_b. leave it alone.

    \_\_\_\_c. add to it.

3. Why should you avoid highlighting or underlining?

    \_\_\_\_a. You are in no position to evaluate what to underline in your initial reading.

    \_\_\_\_b. Highlighting or underlining postpones your learning of the information.

    \_\_\_\_c. None of the above.

4. Why should you take some form of notes when you are study reading?

    \_\_\_\_a. Note taking puts you in a position of responsibility with regard to the information.

    \_\_\_\_b. Note taking requires an immediate and personal response to the information.

    \_\_\_\_c. Note taking can identify any gaps in your learning.

    \_\_\_\_d. Note taking provides a permanent record of the information.

    \_\_\_\_e. All of the above.

    \_\_\_\_f. None of the above.

5. "Reduce and rephrase" means what in terms of note taking?

6. What do you do with the left-hand margin of your notes?

## TECHNICAL READING IN VARIOUS FORMATS

Although the entire study procedure may be necessary for some types of material, most of the time you will selectively apply the steps according to the structure of the material and your reading needs. Whatever your needs and structure, it is vital that you have a consistent method of absorbing the information. Following are some suggestions for applying the study techniques of DC/UR (divide, conquer/unite and rule) to various formats.

*Newspapers.* There are three broad categories of articles: news articles, feature stories, and columns. The structure of the articles is an inverted pyramid, with the most important information presented in the first few paragraphs. Rapid read the first few paragraphs and, if you have time, pick up secondary information from the rest of the article.

*Correspondence/Memos.* Format for correspondence and memos varies so widely, and the quality of writing is so uneven, that it is best to preview the entire piece and mark the main points of the text. Along with marking main points, you may be writing what type of response or follow-up activity is required. You may read and mark if there are procedures outlined. A short VDI at the bottom will save time if you need to follow up.

*Journals.* Survey the entire journal and mark those selections that you wish to spend more time on. In terms of each selection, read the synopsis or beginning and closing paragraphs. Identify those selections that you will need to study read and budget your time accordingly.

*Reports.* The organization of reports is as varied as the subject matter. First, survey to discover how it's organized. Some reports present a great deal of background material that may or may not waste your time. Second, as you consider each report, look for theme, scope, development, and conclusion by reading the summary or synopsis. Then look at the table of contents and appendices. Read the conclusions. If you need to do more in-depth reading, preview the article, selectively marking passages that you might need to study read. A VDI attached to the report can save you time and effort.

## CONCLUSION

The study procedure may seem cumbersome at first, but you will soon see the efficacy of the method after you become familiar with the steps outlined in "Practice Session for the Week." At the beginning of the week, the study procedure is foremost in your mind, but with practice, the steps become readily useful. This focus on the process of study, rather than the content of the material, does not allow you to fully maintain your attention on the material you are trying to read and study. Often the process overshadows the content; but with practice, the method will become an integral part of your learning repertoire. You may discover that, after you are confident with the entire method, you may want to fine-tune the steps according to your materials and purposes.

Learning a logical, systematic, flexible method of acquiring information empowers you with the means of obtaining a limitless storehouse of knowledge. There is no secret to acquiring it in an efficient, pleasant, and interesting manner. It simply requires understanding, motivation, and practice to become a first-rate reader/learner.

The comprehension skills that you have been exposed to in this chapter must be verified by your own reading experiences. They will stand the test of application and give you a most effective tool, if you are willing to invest time and effort in polishing the skills presented in this chapter.

**Chapter 4 Practice Session for the Week**

1. Use your hand in *all* your reading.
2. Practice at least one hour per day.
3. Set yourself a goal for the week and commit yourself to attaining it— minimum is 750 words per minute.

Before beginning your drill, remember to break in your book and practice turning pages for a few minutes.

*DRILL:*

1. Survey and mark off a section of 3,000 words. Set your purpose.
   a. Time/speed goals.
   b. Best comprehension attainable.
2. Preview in one and one-half minutes, using the "S" method. Set up a VDI.
3. Read section in four minutes maximum. Make a VDI. Compute your words per minute and circle this number. Add to the VDI.
4. Reread/Recheck.
5. Add to the VDI.

Repeat this drill in new sections at least 50 minutes per day for six days.

---

**Memo Reading Practice**

Preview the following letters with the "S" pattern. Mark in the margin important points or those points that would require further study reading. Circle anything you need to act upon or respond to. At the bottom of each, design a brief VDI for future reference.

MEGA-BUCKS, INC.
2895 S. Highland Avenue
Norbeck, CA 92003

INTER-OFFICE MEMORANDUM

TO: All Supervisors

FROM: Patsy Rowe, Parking Coordinator

SUBJECT: Garage Maintenance

Due to refurbishment and construction on the second floor of the parking garage, beginning Thursday, October 12, 1981, the following employees will have alternate parking:

| | |
|---|---|
| Vince Benfante | Sara Johnson |
| Nancy Bodwell | Doris Marshall |
| Kirk Brown | Fran McCaag |
| Betty Bruton | Kris Parrott |
| John Clancy | Connie Rief |
| Myrtle Deakins | Kay Rivers |
| Gary Felt | Toni Rodriquez |
| Mike Homcomb | John Sargent |
| Casey Johnson | Penny Taylor |
| Dalene Johnson | |

Please inform the above-listed employees to park on the seventh floor of the parking garage rather than the second floor. This situation is expected to last approximately four weeks. Further notices will keep you informed of any changes.

Thank you for your cooperation.

TO: Bob Sereno

FROM: Linda Hess, President
            Obfuscation, Ltd.

SUBJECT: MEGA-BUCKS, Inc.

The following program design has been forwarded to you for your consideration. We would be pleased to receive the benefit of your present thinking on it as we are giving it active consideration for next year and would appreciate your input concerning the efficacy of its presence at the convention.

If we decide to expedite the development, we will advise in due course after we have gathered the survey results and developed a course of production that will fit into the over-all design of the company's commitment.

MEGA-BUCKS, INC.
2895 S. Highland Avenue
Norbeck, CA 92003

Dear Sirs:

A weekly Weight Reduction Program for interested employees is scheduled to begin at MEGA-BUCKS on Monday, January 22, 1981, at 5:30 p.m., in the President's Lounge, fifth floor of the Cooper Building.

This weight reduction program is designed to help employees lose weight by following a nutritionally balanced, healthful diet.

The first meeting will last 1½ hours, and subsequent meetings will be for 30 minutes. The program will be presented if there is a minimum of 25 employees who attend the first meeting. Motivational and instruction materials are distributed each week and are included in the private course.

The registration fee is $5.00 and each meeting costs $1.00. More information about the program and registration may be obtained by contacting Anna Banana, extention 7616. Mrs. Banana will also assist those people who need to arrange for car pooling.

MEGA-BUCKS, INC.
2895 S. Highland Avenue
Norbeck, CA 92003


TO: X. O. VERISSI

FROM: Bill Overdew

SUBJECT: Plant Visit Follow-Up


We were very pleased to have you visit our plant and wish that more time could have been devoted to discussing the flexible staffing design in more depth. Perhaps when we get together again in August we can do so, with more personnel included in the discussion.

As we mentioned during our conversations, it would be helpful to our sales and promotion departments here in Chicago if, at some time during the next quarter, a training program be delivered on the latest techniques for handling the new Federal regulations that seem to be keeping us flooded with paperwork. Perhaps your staff could design a three- or four-day seminar that would be tailored to the specific needs of our departments. I am sure they would welcome the assistance and realize a new efficiency in the program with your expert help.

Please contact our manager of sales and promotion at your convenience and arrange terms, location, and timing with her. Her name is Suzanna Johnson and her extension is 5705. She has been briefed on your capabilities and will be happy to assist your firm in any way she can.

Once again, thank you for your interesting input concerning our new staffing design and we hope to see you in the future.

MEGA-BUCKS, INC.
2895 S. Highland Avenue
Norbeck, CA 92003


TO WHOM IT MAY CONCERN:


We have received a loan application from one of your employees, named below. We would appreciate it if you would please verify the information. Sign the statement and add any other comments you might have.

Sincerely,


Donald Frey
Loan Officer


Employee Name: Alvin B. Smith
Occupation: Purchasing Supervisor
Length of Service: 7 years
Annual Earnings: $15,700


I certify the above is true. _____

MEGA-BUCKS, INC.
2895 S. Highland Avenue
Norbeck, CA 92003


INTER-OFFICE MEMORANDUM


TO: Mary Jackson

FROM: Wes Barker

SUBJECT: Production


Last year's production reports have just been issued and I can't tell you how pleased we are with the improvement that has come from your department. Greater productivity has long been a need here at MEGA-BUCKS. You have contributed to the company's growth and leadership in the field. All the more reason now to look to the future and decide the possibilities for next quarter's growth. Let's see what we can do to make your outstanding record even more glowing and further the company's remarkable growth. How about 1,000,000 units for the next quarter?

---

**Reading Selection**

There are 4,316 total words in the following article. Use the study procedure to read for good comprehension. Set your own time and speed goals.

# The Effective Decision

Peter Drucker

Decision-making is closely related to problem-solving. The essential difference is that the problem-solver looks for a "right" answer, whereas the decision-maker might have to choose among several "right" answers for the *one that the organization will take action on*. The responsibility for decision-making belongs, of course, to management. But the techniques for decision-making are also important for the engineers, technicians, and scientists who must work at problem-solving, but do not have managerial responsibilities. As Peter Drucker observes, a decision by management has a chance of success only if there is cooperation among all who must work to implement it—including managers and non-managers alike. Although a single person must finally make the decision, he or she needs constructive criticism and suggestions from peers and subordinates. The needed cooperation, support, and constructive criticism are more likely to emerge when key personnel understand that decision-making is a group process, not the boss's whim. It is as a group process that decision-making "mobilizes the vision, energies, and resources of the organization for effective action."

In this selection Peter Drucker discusses some specific approaches to decision-making.

**Facts or Opinions?**

A decision is a judgment. It is a choice between alternatives. It is rarely a choice between right and wrong. It is at best a choice between "almost right" and "probably wrong"—but much more often a choice between two courses of action neither of which is probably more nearly right than the other.

Most books on decision-making tell the reader: "First find the facts." But managers who make effective decisions know that one does not start with facts. One starts with opinions. These are, of course, nothing but untested hypotheses and, as such, worthless unless tested against reality. To determine what is a fact requires first a decision on the criteria of relevance, especially on the appropriate measurement. This is the hinge of the effective decision, and usually its most controversial aspect.

But also, the effective decision does not, as so many tests on decision-making proclaim, flow from a "consensus on the facts." The understanding that underlies the right decision grows out of the clash and conflict of divergent opinions and out of the serious consideration of competing alternatives.

To get the facts first is impossible. There are no facts unless one has a criterion of relevance. Events by themselves are not facts.

Only by starting out with opinions can the decision-maker find out what the decision is all about. People do, of course, differ in the answers they give. But most differences of opinion reflect an underlying—and usually hidden— difference as to what the decision is actually about. They reflect a difference regarding the question that has to be answered. Thus to identify the alternative questions is the first step in making effective decisions.

Conversely, there are few things as futile—and as damaging—as the right answer to the wrong question.

The effective decision-maker also knows that he starts out with opinions anyhow. The only choice he has is between using opinions as a productive factor in the decision-making process and deceiving himself into false objectivity. People do not start out with the search for facts. They start out with an opinion. There is nothing wrong with this. People experienced in an area should be expected to have an opinion. Not to have an opinion after having been exposed to an area for a good long time would argue an unobservant eye and a sluggish mind.

People inevitably start out with an opinion; to ask them to search for the facts first is even undesirable. They will simply do what everyone is far too prone to do anyhow: look for the facts that fit the conclusion they have already reached. And no one has ever failed to find the facts he is looking for. The good statistician knows this and distrusts all figures—he either knows the fellow who found them or he does not know him; in either case he is suspicious.

The only rigorous method, the only one that enables us to test an opinion against reality, is based on the clear recognition that opinions come first—and that is the way it should be. Then no one can fail to see that we start out with untested hypotheses—in decision-making, as in science, the only starting point. We know what to do with hypotheses. One does not argue them; one tests them. One finds out which hypotheses are tenable, and therefore worthy of serious considerations, and which are eliminated by the first test against observable experience.

The effective decision-maker therefore encourages opinions. But he insists that the people who voice them also think through what it is that the "experiment"—that is, the testing of the opinion against reality—would have to show. The effective executive, therefore, asks, "What do we have to know to test the validity of this hypothesis?" "What would the facts have to be to make this opinion tenable?" And he makes it a habit—in himself and in the people with whom he works—to think through and spell out what needs to be looked at, studied, and tested. He insists that people who voice an opinion also take responsibility for defining what factual findings can be expected and should be looked for.

Perhaps the crucial question here is "What is the measurement appropriate to the matter under discussion and to the decision to be reached?" Whenever one analyzes the way a truly effective, a truly right, decision has been reached, one finds that a great deal of work and thought went into finding the appropriate measurement.

### The Need for Dissent and Alternatives

Unless one has considered alternatives, one has a closed mind. This, above all, explains why the Japanese deliberately disregard the second major command of the textbooks on decision-making and create discussion and dissent as a means to consensus.

Decisions of the kind the executive has to make are not made well by acclamation. They are made well only if based on the clash of conflicting views, the dialogue between different points of view, the choice between different judgments. The first rule in decision-making is that one does not make a decision unless there is disagreement.

Alfred P. Sloan, Jr., is reported to have said at a meeting of one of the GM top committees, "Gentlemen, I take it we are all in complete agreement on the decision here." Everyone around the table nodded assent. "Then," continued Mr. Sloan, "I propose we postpone further discussion of this matter until our next meeting to give ourselves time to develop disagreement and perhaps gain some understanding of what the decision is all about."

Sloan was anything but an "intuitive" decision-maker. He always emphasized the need to test opinions against facts and the need to make absolutely sure that one did not start out with the conclusion and then look for the facts that would support it. But he knew that the right decision demands adequate disagreement.

Every one of the effective presidents in American history had its own method of producing the disagreement he needed in order to make an effective decision. Washington, we know, hated conflicts and quarrels and wanted a united Cabinet. Yet he made quite sure of the necessary differences of opinion on important matters by asking both Hamilton and Jefferson for their opinions.

There are three reasons why dissent is needed. It first safeguards the decision-maker against becoming the prisoner of the organization. Everybody always wants something from the decision-maker. Everybody is a special pleader, trying—often in perfectly good faith—to obtain the decision he favors. This is true whether the decision-maker is the president of the United States or the most junior engineer working on a design modification.

The only way to break out of the prison of special pleading and preconceived notions is to make sure of argued, documented, thought-through disagreements.

Second, disagreement alone can provide alternatives to a decision. And a decision without an alternative is a desperate gambler's throw, no matter how carefully thought through it might be. There is always a high possibility that the decision will prove wrong—either because it was wrong to begin with or because a change in circumstances makes it wrong. If one has thought through alternatives during the decision-making process, one has something to fall back on, something that has already been thought through, studied, understood. Without such an alternative, one is likely to flounder dismally when reality proves a decision to be inoperative.

Both the Schlieffen Plan of the German Army in 1914 and President Franklin D. Roosevelt's original economic program in 1933 were disproved by events at the very moment when they should have taken effect.

The German Army never recovered. It never formulated another strategic concept. It went from one ill-conceived improvisation to the next. But this was inevitable. For twenty-five years no alternatives to the Schlieffen Plan had been considered by the General Staff. All its skills had gone into working out the details of this master plan. When the plan fell to pieces, no one had an alternative to fall back on. All the German generals could do, therefore, was gamble—with the odds against them.

By contrast, President Roosevelt, who, in the months before he took office, had based his whole campaign on the slogan of economic orthodoxy, had a team of able people, the later "Brain Trust," working on an alternative—a radical policy based on the proposals of the old-time Progressives, and aimed at economic and social reform on a grand scale. When the collapse of the banking system made it clear that economic orthodoxy had become political suicide, Roosevelt had his alternative ready. He therefore had a policy.

Above all, disagreement is needed to stimulate the imagination. One may not need imagination to find the *one right* solution to a problem. But then this is of value only in mathematics. In all matters of true uncertainty such as the executive deals with—whether his sphere be political, economic, social, or military—one needs creative solutions which create a new situation. And this means that one needs imagination—a new and different way of perceiving and understanding.

Imagination of the first order is, I admit, not in abundant supply. But neither is it as scarce as is commonly believed. Imagination needs to be challenged and stimulated, however, or else it remains latent and unused. Disagreement, especially if forced to be reasoned, thought through, documented, is the most effective stimulus we know.

The effective decision-maker, therefore, organizes dissent. This protects him against being taken in by the plausible but false or incomplete. It gives him the alternatives so that he can choose and make a decision, but also ensures that he is not lost in the fog when his decision proves deficient or wrong in execution. And it forces the imagination—his own and that of his associates. Dissent converts the plausible into the right and the right into the good decision.

### The Trap of "Being Right"

The effective decision-maker does not start out with the assumption that one proposed course of action is right and that all others must be wrong. Nor does he start out with the assumption "I am right and he is wrong." He starts out with the commitment to find out why people disagree.

Effective executives know, of course, that there are fools around and that there are mischief-makers. But they do not assume that the man who disagrees with what they themselves see as clear and obvious is, therefore, either a fool or a knave. They know that unless proven otherwise, the dissenter has to be assumed to be reasonably intelligent and reasonably fair-minded. Therefore, it has to be assumed that he has reached his so obviously wrong conclusion because he sees a different reality and is concerned with a different problem. The effective executive, therefore, always asks, "What does this fellow have to see if his position were, after all, tenable, rational, intelligent?" The effective executive is concerned first with *understanding*. Only then does he even think about who is right and who is wrong.

Needless to say, this is not done by a great many people, whether executives or not. Most people start out with the certainty that how they see is the only way to see at all. As a result, they never understand what the decision—and indeed the whole argument—is really all about.

The American steel executives have never asked the question "Why do these union people get so terribly upset every time we mention the word 'featherbedding'?" The union people in turn have never asked themselves why steel managements make such a fuss over featherbedding when every single instance thereof they have ever produced has proved to be petty, and irrelevant to boot. Instead, both sides have worked mightily to prove each other wrong. If either side had tried to understand what the other one sees and why, both would be a great deal stronger, and labor relations in the steel industry, if not in U.S. industry, might be a good deal healthier.

No matter how high his emotions run, no matter how certain he is that the other side is completely wrong and has no case at all, the executive who wants to make the right decision forces himself to see opposition as *his* means to think through the alternatives. He uses conflict of opinion as his tool to make sure all major aspects of an important matter are looked at carefully.

### Is a Decision Necessary?

There is one question the effective decision-maker asks: "Is a decision really necessary?" *One* alternative is always the alternative of doing nothing.

One has to make a decision when a condition is likely to degenerate if nothing is done. This also applies with respect to opportunity. If the opportunity is important and is likely to vanish unless one acts with dispatch, one acts—and one makes a radical change.

Theodore Vail's contemporaries agreed with him as to the degenerative danger of government ownership; but they wanted to fight it by fighting symptoms—fighting this or that bill in the legislature, opposing this or that candidate and supporting another, and so on. Vail alone understood that this is the ineffectual way to fight a degenerative condition. Even if one wins every battle, one can never win the war. He saw that drastic action was needed to create a new situation. He alone saw that private business had to make public regulation into an effective alternative to nationalization.

At the opposite end there are those conditions with respect to which one can, without being unduly optimistic, expect that they will take care of themselves even if nothing is done. If the answer to the question "What will happen if we do nothing?" is "It will take care of itself," one does not interfere. Nor does one interfere if the condition, while annoying, is of no importance and unlikely to make much difference.

It is a rare executive who understands this. The controller who in a financial crisis preaches cost reduction is seldom capable of leaving alone minor blemishes, elimination of which will achieve nothing. He may know, for instance, that the significant costs are in the sales organization and in physical distribution. And he will work hard and brilliantly at getting them under control. But then he will discredit himself and the whole effort by making a big fuss about the "unnecessary" employment of two or three old men in an otherwise efficient and well-run plant. And he will dismiss as immoral the argument that eliminating these few semipensioners will not make any difference anyhow. "Other people are making sacrifices," he will argue. "Why should the plant people get away with inefficiency?"

When it is all over, the organization will forget that he saved the business. They will remember, though, his vendetta against the two or three poor devils in the plant—and rightly so. *De minimis non curat praetor* (The magistrate does not consider trifles) said the Roman law almost two thousand years ago—but many decision-makers still need to learn it.

The great majority of decisions will lie between these extremes. The problem is not going to take care of itself; but it is unlikely to turn into degenerative malignancy either. The opportunity is only for improvement rather than for real change and innovation; but it is still quite considerable. If we do not act, in other words, we will in all probability survive. But if we do act, we may be better off.

In this situation the effective decision-maker compares effort and risk of action to risk of inaction. There is no formula for the right decision here. But the guidelines are so clear that decision in the concrete case is rarely difficult.

They are:
   —act if on balance the benefits greatly outweight cost and risk; and
   —act or do not act; but do not "hedge" or compromise.

The surgeon who takes out only half the tonsils or half the appendix risks as much infection and shock as if he did the whole job. And he has not cured the condition, has indeed made it worse. He either operates or he doesn't. Similarly, the effective decision-maker either acts or he doesn't act. He does not take half-action. This is the one thing that is always wrong.

### Who Has to Do the Work?

When they reach this point, most decision-makers in the West think they can make an effective decision. But, as the Japanese example shows, one essential element is still missing. An effective decision is a commitment to action and results. If it has to be "sold" *after* it has been made, there will be no action and no results—and, in effect, no decision. At the least, there may be so much delay as to obsolete the decision before it has become truly effective.

The first rule is to make sure that everyone who will have to do something to make the decision effective—or who could sabotage it—has been forced to participate responsibly in the discussion. This is not "democracy." It is salesmanship.

But it is equally important to build the action commitments into the decision from the start. In fact, no decision has been made unless carrying it out in specific steps has become someone's work assignment and responsibility. Until then, there are only good intentions.

This is the trouble with so many policy statements, especially of business: they contain no action commitment. To carry them out is no one's specific work and responsibility. No wonder that the people in the organization tend to view these statements cynically if not as declarations of what top management is really not going to do.

Converting a decision into action requires answering several distinct questions: "Who has to know of this decision?" "What action has to be taken?" "Who is to take it?" "And what does the action have to be so that the people who have to do it *can* do it?" The first and the last of these are too often overlooked—with dire results.

A story that has become a legend among management scientists illustrates the importance of the question "Who has to know?" A major manufacturer of industrial equipment decided to discontinue one model. For years it had been standard equipment on a line of machine tools, many of which were still in use. It was decided, therefore, to sell the model to present owners of the old equipment for another three years, as a replacement, and then to stop making and selling it. Orders for this particular model had been going down for a good many years. But they shot up temporarily as former customers reordered against the day when the model would no longer be available. No one had, however, asked, "Who needs to know of this decision?" Therefore nobody informed the clerk in the purchasing department who was in charge of buying the parts from which the model itself was being assembled. His instructions were to buy parts in a given ratio to current sales—and the instructions remained unchanged. When the time came to discontinue further production of the model, the company had in its warehouse enough parts for another eight to ten years of production, parts that had to be written off at a considerable loss.

Above all, the action must be appropriate to the capacities of the people who have to carry it out.

A chemical company found itself, in the early sixties, with fairly large amounts of blocked currency in two West African countries. To protect this money, it decided to invest in local business which would contribute to the local economy, would not require imports from abroad, and would, if successful, be the kind that could be sold to local investors if and when currency remittances became possible again. To establish these businesses, the company developed a simple chemical process to preserve a tropical fruit which is a staple crop in both countries and which, up until then, had suffered serious spoilage in transit to its markets.

The business was a success in both countries. But in one country the local manager set the business up in such a manner that it required highly skilled and, above all, technically trained management of the kind not easily available in West Africa. In the other country the local manager thought through the capacities of the people who would eventually have to run the business and worked hard at making both process and business simple and at staffing from the start with nationals of the country right up to the top.

A few years later it became possible again to transfer currency from these two countries. But though the business flourished, no buyer could be found for it in the first country. No one available locally had the necessary managerial and technical skills. The business had to be liquidated at a loss. In the other country so many local entrepreneurs were eager to buy the business that the company repatriated its original investment with a substantial profit.

The process and the business built on it were essentially the same in both places. But in the first country no one had asked, "What kind of people do we have available to make this decision effective? And what can they do?" As a result, the decision itself became frustrated.

All this becomes doubly important when people have to change behavior, habits, or attitudes if a decision is to become effective action. Here one has to make sure not only that responsibility for the action is clearly assigned and that the people responsible are capable of doing the needful. One has to make sure that their measurements, their standards for accomplishment, and their incentives are changed simultaneously. Otherwise, the people will get caught in a paralyzing internal emotional conflict.

Theodore Vail's decision that the business of the Bell System was service might have remained dead letter but for the yardsticks of service performance which he designed to measure managerial performance. Bell managers were used to being measured by the profitability of their units, or at the least, by cost. The new yardsticks made them accept rapidly the new objectives.

If the greatest rewards are given for behavior contrary to that which the new course of action requires, then everyone will conclude that this contrary behavior is what the people at the top really want and are going to reward.

Not everyone can do what Vail did and build the execution of his decisions into the decision itself. But everyone can think through what action commitments a specific decision requires, what work assignment follows from it, and what people are available to carry it out.

### The Right and the Wrong Compromise

The decision is now ready to be made. The specifications have been thought through, the alternatives explored, the risks and gains weighed. Who will have to do what is understood. At this point it is indeed reasonably clear what course of action should be taken. At this point the decision does indeed almost "make itself."

And it is at this point that most decisions are lost. It becomes suddenly quite obvious that the decision is not going to be pleasant, is not going to be popular, is not going to be easy. It becomes clear that a decision requires courage as much as it requires judgment. There is no inherent reason why medicines should taste horrible—but effective ones usually do. Similarly, there is no inherent reason why decisions should be distasteful—but most effective ones are.

The reason is always the same: there is no "perfect" decision. One always has to pay a price. One has always to subordinate one set of *desiderata*. One always has to balance conflicting objectives, conflicting opinions, and conflicting priorities. The best decision is only an approximation—and a risk. And there is always the pressure to compromise to gain acceptance, to placate strong opponents of the proposed course of action or to hedge risks.

To make effective decisions under such circumstances requires starting out with a firm commitment to what is right rather than with the question "Who is right?" One has to compromise in the end. But unless one starts out with the closest one can come to the decision that will truly satisfy objective requirements, one ends up with the wrong compromise—the compromise that abandons essentials.

For there are two different kinds of compromise. One kind is expressed in the old proverb "Half a loaf is better than no bread." The other kind is expressed in the story of the Judgment of Solomon, which was clearly based on the realization that "half a baby is worse than no baby at all." In the first instance, objective requirements are still being satisfied. The purpose of bread is to provide food, and half a loaf is still food. Half a baby, however, is not half of a living and growing child. It is a corpse in two pieces.

It is, above all, fruitless and a waste of time to worry about what is acceptable and what one had better not say so as not to evoke resistance. The things one worries about never happen. And objections and difficulties no one thought about suddenly turn out to be almost insurmountable obstacles. One gains nothing, in other words, by starting out with the question "What is acceptable?" And in the process of answering it, one loses any chance to come up with an effective, let alone with the right, answer.

### The Feedback

A feedback has to be built into the decision to provide continuous testing, against actual events, of the expectations that underlie the decision. Few decisions work out the way they are intended to. Even the best decision usually runs into snags, unexpected obstacles, and all kinds of surprises. Even the most effective decision eventually becomes obsolete. Unless there is feedback from the results of a decision, it is unlikely to produce the desired results.

This requires first that the expectations be spelled out clearly—and in writing. Second, it requires an organized effort to follow up. And this feedback is part of the decision and has to be worked out in the decision process.

When General Eisenhower was elected president, his predecessor, Harry Truman, said: "Poor Ike; when he was a general, he gave an order and it was carried out. Now he is going to sit in that big office and he'll give an order and not a damn thing is going to happen."

The reason why "not a damn thing is going to happen" is, however, not that generals have more authority than presidents. It is that military organizations learned long ago that futility is the lot of most orders and organized the feedback, to check on the execution of the order. They learned long ago that to go oneself and look is the only reliable feedback. Reports—all an American president is normally able to mobilize—are not much help. All military services have long ago learned that the officer who has given an order goes out and sees for himself whether it has been carried out. At the least he sends one of his own aides—he never relies on what he is told by the subordinate to whom the order was given. Not that he distrusts the subordinate; he has learned from experience to distrust communications.

One needs organized information for the feedback. One needs reports and figures. But unless one builds one's feedback around direct exposure to reality— unless one disciplines oneself to go out and look—one condemns oneself to sterile dogmatism and with it to ineffectiveness.

In sum: decision-making is not a mechanical job. It is risk-taking and a challenge to judgment. The "right answer" (which usually cannot be found anyway) is not central. Central is understanding of the problem. Decision-making, further, is not an intellectual exercise. It mobilizes the vision, energies, and resources of the organization for effective action.

**Drucker Comprehension Questions**

1. According to Drucker, why should the opinion-maker start with opinions rather than facts?

2. How are unsound opinions eliminated?

3. Why are dissent and alternatives important in decision-making?

4. Under what circumstances might we decide to make no decision?

5. Why must a "feed-back" be built into a decision? How do military commanders insure that decisions are carried out?

## ANSWERS

**Progress Check 1**

1. You must have an outward display of the information, i.e., simple repetition to in-depth critical reading.

2. a. quality of perception.
   b. speed.
   c. motivation.
   d. concentration.
   e. well-defined purpose.
   f. retention.
   g. general background.
   h. nature of the material.

3. a. loosely-structured, a story-line.
   b. more structured, more information per page, systematic movement from concepts to supportive data, a greater personal responsibility towards the material.

**Progress Check 2**

1. In order to be efficient, you need an organized procedure that is flexible.
2. Good division means sensitivity organization, clear purpose, realistic goals.
3. Read everything carefully and deliberately, noting emphasis, relationships, and prior knowledge.
4. Uniting prepares for accurate remembering.
5. Selection, anticipation.
6. Both do not require wholesale absorption.

**Progress Check 3**

1. b.
2. a,b,c,d.
3. Everything seems important, whether it is or not.
4. b,c.

**Progress Check 4**

1. overview, larger meaningful perspective.
2. a,c.
3. uses closure to make your brain eager to comprehend.

4. By moving quickly and efficiently through the material you can assure yourself you know it, *or* that you may have to study harder. It also helps for prudent goal and purpose definition.
5. A good survey helps you to refine your goals.
6. 50 ... 10.
7. a,b.

## Progress Check 5

1. Three to five times your reading rate.
2. "S."
3. main ideas.
4. f.
5. Proper questions help focus on pertinent information.

## Progress Check 6

1. fast enough to keep you from losing concentration, slow enough to satisfy your purpose.
2. study read to answer those questions.
3. it wastes your time and may mislead you later on.
4. checks and symbols in the margin.

## Progress Check 7

1. b.
2. a,b,c.
3. a,b.
4. e.
5. Put the information in your own words and be concise.
6. List the key words or phrases from your notes.

**ANSWERS: Drucker Article**

1. Only by beginning with opinions can the decision-maker find out what the decision is all about. You only start out with opinions anyway, and people tend to look for the facts that fit a conclusion they have already reached.
2. by testing them against observable appearance.
3. First they safeguard the decision-maker from becoming a prisoner of the organization; next, disagreement provides alternatives; and finally, it stimulates imagination.
4. if the situation will take care of itself, even if nothing is done.
5. to provide continuous testing against actual events, of expectations that underlie the decision. Unless there is feedback, it is unlikely to produce the desired results.
   They go and look for themselves.

## ONE WEEK'S PRACTICE RECORD

FROM _____ TO _____
      date              date

| | | | |
|---|---|---|---|
| **1st Session** | Highest PR:____wpm | Highest R:____wpm | Name of Book:_____ _____ |
| total # of mins._____ | Lowest PR:____wpm | Lowest R:____wpm | Comments: |
| **2nd Session** | Highest PR:____wpm | Highest R:____wpm | Name of Book:_____ _____ |
| total # of mins._____ | Lowest PR:____wpm | Lowest R:____wpm | Comments: |
| **3rd Session** | Highest PR:____wpm | Highest R:____wpm | Name of Book:_____ _____ |
| total # of mins._____ | Lowest PR:____wpm | Lowest R:____wpm | Comments: |
| **4th Session** | Highest PR:____wpm | Highest R:____wpm | Name of Book:_____ _____ |
| total # of mins._____ | Lowest PR:____wpm | Lowest R:____wpm | Comments: |
| **5th Session** | Highest PR:____wpm | Highest R:____wpm | Name of Book:_____ _____ |
| total # of mins._____ | Lowest PR:____wpm | Lowest R:____wpm | Comments: |
| **6th Session** | Highest PR:____wpm | Highest R:____wpm | Name of Book:_____ _____ |
| total # of mins._____ | Lowest PR:____wpm | Lowest R:____wpm | Comments: |
| **7th Session** | Highest PR:____wpm | Highest R:____wpm | Name of Book:_____ _____ |
| total # of mins._____ | Lowest PR:____wpm | Lowest R:____wpm | Comments: |
| **8th Session** | Highest PR:____wpm | Highest R:____wpm | Name of Book:_____ _____ |
| total # of mins._____ | Lowest PR:____wpm | Lowest R:____wpm | Comments: |

SUMMARY

| TOTAL TIME | Highest PR:____wpm Highest Read:_____ |
|---|---|
| ☐ | Lowest PR:____wpm Lowest Read:_____ |
| | Comments: |

128

# 5 ——————— Developing Concentration

## WHAT IS GOOD CONCENTRATION?

If your mind wanders to thoughts other than those inspired by the page while you are reading (e.g., What am I going to have for lunch? What will I wear tonight? What are we going to do this weekend? How will the meeting go this afternoon?) then you know what it is like to have poor concentration. Most readers express as much concern with their poor concentration abilities as with their poor reading speeds, and rightly so, because the two are closely interrelated. However, when asked to define concentration, most people have only a vague understanding of what good reading concentration is.

On the other hand, most of us have had the enjoyable experience of total immersion in something, to the point of being oblivious to the external environment. Whether this was a hobby or a particularly challenging problem at work, that unique and satisfying absorption is a useful tool to carry over into the reading experience. This absorbtion, or as Webster defines it, "...the direction of your attention," is a skill that can be cultivated and improved with knowledge and practice.

Good concentration in reading, or the ability to keep your attention focused upon what you desire, is particularly encouraged by the new speed and comprehension skills you have been learning. Both the speed and comprehension skills require you to become actively involved in the reading process in many ways. These skills require personal and evaluative involvement, from decisions about how fast you will read, to deciding your purpose in reading, to how your VDI will be constructed. In fact, nothing enhances a good concentration environment more than a personal, active involvement in the material.

Recent studies have concluded that when you involve as many of your five senses as possible with a learning situation, the better your concentration in that learning situation will be. By using your hand as a pacer, you have brought in the tactile sense. This does not mean that the words are siphoned through your index finger, along your arm, into your brain. It does mean, though, that your focus of attention has another means of keeping it correctly located. Your hand touching the page tends to keep your concentration focused on the page as well.

The study technique you learned in the last chapter contains many activities to enhance your concentration ability. The thorough preview allows your mind to get ready to concentrate as you begin to assess your reading task. Previewing for the main ideas sensitizes you to the type, amount, and difficulty of the material and discloses the overall pattern of information. Breaking the material into manageable pieces allows your concentration to be high at the appropriate times and places. Note taking and evaluation of the material brings into play other contexts from which the material can be viewed. These activities, when combined, allow your concentration to change tempo, intensity, and perspective, which will keep your concentration appropriately intense.

As discussed in Chapter 2, your reading speed influences your concentration. If you are not giving your brain enough work to do, it will find activities of its own while you are trying to read. Most of our students immediately notice a heightened sense of concentration when they begin to read faster.

## TIPS FOR IMPROVING CONCENTRATION

Along with the new speed and comprehension techniques that aid your concentration, you can do some other things to improve your mind's ability to stay directed focused on what you want. Since directing your attention is the key concept in concentration, internal and external distractions are of concern in your efforts to improve concentration skills. The following tips can improve your concentration by eliminating or reducing those external and internal distractions that could ruin a good opportunity for reading and study.

### PREPARE YOURSELF TO CONCENTRATE BEFORE YOU BEGIN TO READ

By scheduling your reading time, you can begin a great deal of work before you actually start. Make an appointment with yourself to sit down and read with good concentration. This will start your mind to work on that activity long before you actually sit down to read. Make a point of thinking about concentrating before you are scheduled to read.

### AVOID EXTERNAL DISTRACTION

Some distractions in your external environment can be controlled, some cannot. While we wish you could live in a perfect work/study world, we know that it is not entirely possible. Therefore, the suggestions discussed here are ideal; it is your job to move toward the ideal concentration environment as best you can. Also, be aware that you may be setting yourself up for external distraction if your desire to read is minimal. Be honest with yourself about how many external distractions you can eliminate. Carefully assess if those distractions that are "impossible" to eliminate are really signs that you do not want to read something in the first place.

### Find the Right Place

Eliminate visual distractions. You may think that a neat desk with no distracting clutter will only get you the "Neat-As-A-Pin Award." Actually, a neat desk with no other materials, other than what you are going to read, also helps you concentrate better.

### Eliminate Unplanned Interruptions

Place yourself out of the proximity of phones (don't you wish), areas of high traffic, and away from your children. This means that before you start, you will have all your required materials in front of you so you won't have to jump up and find that missing weekly staff report. Placing yourself in the position of having to run around looking for something breaks concentration.

### Eliminate Aural Distractions

Some people require complete silence when they concentrate. That may be impractical at times, as complete silence exists in few places in our society. Therefore, *any* sound such as sirens or someone coughing, would break concentration. On the other hand, some people think that sitting in the middle of a rock concert helps them concentrate. Yet very loud music tends to exhaust the concentration level quite soon. Neither environment helps concentration. The best aural environment has some type of quiet masking or "white noise" to eliminate the ordinary noises. A good example is the sound of an aquarium pump bubbling in the room. Soft music without too many commercial interruptions, or a running air conditioner are also good aural concentration aids.

### Find the Right Time

Everyone experiences mental highs and lows throughout the day. Some people find they can get a great deal of work done before the rest of the world is awake. Other people need a jump-start to get their hearts beating before noon. Still others find the early evening is their mental high point. If you are not aware of the fluctuation of your concentration's strength, make a point to discover it in the next few days. Sometimes you have no choice about times to read with good concentration. However, if you have an opportunity to choose when you will read, that is the time to be aware of when your concentration level is apt to be the highest.

It is also possible to develop special periods of high concentration by setting aside time each day to give all your attention to reading. The key here is to be consistent with that reading time. Your mind will become positively conditioned as you develop the habit of good concentration at that particular time of day.

## Set Goals

Concentration improves with correct assessment of purpose and with definite speed and time goals incorporated into your reading sessions. If you have set a reasonable task with a definite beginning, middle, and end to your reading sessions, then you can more easily put aside other external considerations for the time, freeing your attention for the printed matter at hand.

All of the preceding discussion has been concerned with building an external environment to foster good concentration. These features are somewhat easier to adjust to than internal distractions affecting your ability to concentrate. Your goal for internal distractions is to reduce them to a manageable level if they seem to be contributors to a low concentration level.

## REDUCE INTERNAL DISTRACTIONS

### Don't Procrastinate—DO IT NOW

Putting off reading tasks you know you must do right away can be a debilitating blow to your concentration level. The usual products of procrastination are guilt and anxiety. These feelings depress your ability to concentrate on the material. Some people like to work under pressure, but an inordinate amount of pressure to absorb written material focuses your attention on feelings of guilt, anxiety, and pressure, rather than on the task at hand. Moreover, how can you estimate just the right amount of pressure that will cause higher concentration? It seems like a risk most prudent readers would prefer to avoid.

### Anxieties

If your life is full of anxiety and uncertainty, then your ability to concentrate is hampered. No one's life is entirely free of the typical stresses of work, home, etc., but if you find you are going through unusually stressful periods, you must stop trying to concentrate on printed material and deal with the immediate problems. Or else, try to put them on hold for a while, promising yourself that they will be there when you're done with your task.

## Lack of Self-Discipline

Some people have never been able to concentrate because no one ever required it. Thus, they find it difficult to sit down with a task and complete it with reasonable success. This need not be the case. Given a sincere desire to learn better concentration skills, along with proper, habitual practice routines, concentration can measurably improve.

## Negative Attitude

You may not be thrilled with the material you must read. You may not agree with the author, or you just may not care. All of these negative attitudes detract from your ability to concentrate. If you are attacked with a severe case of "bad attitude," realize that the job must be done and that you are the only one who can do it. You may need to force yourself to work at concentrating for a while, but if you keep in mind the tips in this chapter, you will notice results, even if you must force yourself. Another way to alleviate your negative attitude is to talk to someone who does care. Enthusiasm is contagious. You may find some reason to care by having a conversation with someone who sees value in the material you need to read.

## Mental Fatigue

Most people demand much longer periods of concentration than they are capable of. Some people think the best way to overcome mental fatigue is to work harder. This is illogical and impractical. The best way to avoid mental fatigue is to use the 50-minute hour as described earlier. Studies show that 50 minutes is a good segment of time to maintain good reading/concentration skills. The 10-minute break allows your mind to rest and recoup. Another method to avoid fatigue is to vary the types of information you must read. The change of pace, as well as moving from the easiest to the hardest information, helps concentration levels. If you can arrange it, save the most enjoyable task for last. Use it as a reward for diligent study and concentration.

## Build Concentration Stamina

Many people require high levels of concentration in sporadic reading sessions. As with any skill, concentration can be improved with practice, but you also need to develop the length of your concentration. It has been speculated that the average concentration span in a college classroom is 17 seconds. That means people who demand hours and hours of high concentration from themselves are unrealistic. Practice concentrating with the steps outlined in the weekly practice session at the end of this chapter. Prepare to concentrate, avoid external distractions, reduce internal distractions, and build your concentration stamina. Extend the amount of time you demand concentration from yourself during the week's practice, until you can expect to direct all your attention to your reading material for as long as necessary.

**Progress Check**

1. Concentration, as Webster defines it, is the

2. Using your hand as a pacer improves concentration because:

_____a. it speeds up your reading

_____b. it siphons the words off the page directly into your brain

_____c. it impresses people at parties

_____d. it gives you a point of focus on the page.

3. The study procedure outlined in Chapter 4 enhances concentration because:

_____a. the preview allows you to get ready to concentrate

_____b. selection by proper division of the material breaks the information into manageable pieces

_____c. the VDI allows you to see the information in different and creative contexts.

_____d. none of the above

_____e. all of the above.

4. Identify three personal external distractions.

5. Identify three personal internal distractions.

6. Formulate a personal plan of action for assuaging or eliminating some of your personal distractions.

---

### Reading Selection

Use the following article to implement the tips for better concentration. Remember to:

- get ready to concentrate
- avoid external distractions
- reduce internal distractions
- build your concentration stamina

Apply the procedure as outlined in Chapter 4:

1. Survey. Discover the organization of the article and look at the diagrams.

2. Assess your purpose. One primary purpose in this exercise is to have greater concentration. Check the Assessment of Purpose on page 86 in Chapter 4 for additional options.

3. Set speed goals. There are 1,920 total words. Time yourself at three to five times your study speed.

4. Preview and set up VDI.

5. Study read and make notes.

6. Reread and recheck; add to your notes.

# Thinking by Visual Images

Robert H. McKim

Most of us are probably not aware of just how much of our thinking is visual. McKim alerts us to the role of visual imagery in thinking, and discusses some of the ways that "seeing" helps in problem-solving.

### Visual Thinking Is Pervasive

Visual thinking pervades all human activity, from the abstract and theoretical to the down-to-earth and everyday. An astronomer ponders a mysterious cosmic event; a football coach considers a new strategy; a motorist maneuvers his car along an unfamiliar freeway: all are thinking visually. You are in the midst of a dream; you are planning what to wear today; you are making order out of the disarray on your desk: *you* are thinking visually.

Surgeons think visually to perform an operation; chemists to construct molecular models; mathematicians to consider abstract space-time relationships; engineers to design circuits, structures, and mechanisms; businessmen to organize and schedule work; architects to coordinate function with beauty; carpenters and mechanics to translate plans into things.

Visual thinking, then, is not the exclusive reserve of artists. As Arnheim[1] observes, "Visual thinking is constantly used by everybody. It directs figures on a chessboard and designs global politics on the geographical map. Two dexterous moving-men steering a piano along a winding staircase think visually in an intricate sequence of lifting, shifting, and turning....An inventive housewife transforms an uninviting living room into a room for living by judiciously placing lamps and rearranging couches and chairs."

### See/Imagine/Draw

Visual thinking is carried on by three kinds of visual imagery:
1. the kind that we *see* "People see images, not things."[2]
2. the kind that we *imagine* in our mind's eye, as when we dream.
3. the kind that we *draw,* doodle, or paint.

Although visual thinking can occur primarily in the context of seeing, or only in imagination, or largely with pencil and paper, the expert visual thinker flexibly utilizes all three kinds of imagery. He finds that seeing, imagining, and drawing are interactive.

## Interactive Imagery

The interactive nature of seeing, imagining, and drawing is shown diagrammatically in Figure 1. The overlapping circles can be taken to represent a wide

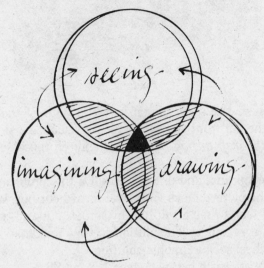

Figure 1.

variety of interactions. Where seeing and drawing overlap, seeing facilitates drawing, while drawing invigorates seeing. Where drawing and imagining overlap, drawing stimulates and expresses imagining, while imagining provides impetus and material for drawing. Where imagining and seeing overlap, imagination directs and filters seeing, while seeing, in turn, provides raw material for imagining. The three overlapping circles symbolize the idea that visual thinking is experienced to the fullest when seeing, imagining, and drawing merge into active interplay.

The visual thinker utilizes seeing, imagining, and drawing in a fluid and dynamic way, moving from one kind of imagery to another. For example, he *sees* a problem from several angles and perhaps even chooses to solve it in the direct context of seeing. Now prepared with a visual understanding of the problem, he *imagines* alternative solutions. Rather than trust to memory, he *draws* a few quick sketches, which he can later evaluate and compare. Cycling between perceptual, inner, and graphic images, he continues until the problem is solved. Experience this interplay between perceptual, inner, and graphic images for yourself, as you solve this challenging and somewhat difficult classic puzzle:

### 1-1/Pierced Block

Figure 2 shows a solid block that has been pierced with circular, triangular, and square holes. The circle's diameter, the triangle's altitude and base, and the

Figure 2.

square's sides all have the same dimension. The walls of the three holes are perpendicular to the flat front face of the block. Visualize a single, solid object that will pass *all the way through* each hole and, en route, entirely block the passage of light.

Use seeing, imagining, and drawing to solve this problem, as follows:

1. Simulate the pierced block with a cardboard cut-out. With scissors and cardboard, seek to see a solution by actual "cut-and-try" methods.
2. Close your eyes and seek a solution in your imagination.
3. Make sketches; seek a graphic solution.
4. Consciously alternate between steps 1, 2, and 3.

(An answer to this puzzle is illustrated at the end of this chapter.)

Visual thinking isobviously central to the practice of architecture, design, and the visual arts. Less obvious is the importance of visual thinking to other disciplines, such as science and technology. In the next few pages I will present a few brief accounts of seeing, imagining, and drawing in the thinking of scientists and technologists. Interspersed with these, I have placed related problems that will help you to relate these accounts of others to your own experience.

## Seeing and Thinking

Discoveries in the direct context of seeing are common in the history of science. For example, Sir Alexander Fleming "was working with some plate cultures of staphylococci which he had occasion to open several times and, as often happens in such circumstances, they became contaminated. He noticed that the colonies of staphylococci around one particular colony had died. Many bacteriologists would not have thought this particularly remarkable for it has long been known that some bacteria interfere with growth of others. Fleming, however, saw the possible significance of the observation and followed it up to discover penicillin."[3]

Why did Fleming discover penicillin when another scientist saw it and considered it only a nuisance? Because habits of seeing and thinking are intimately related. Fleming, like most creative observers, possessed a habit of mind that permitted him to see things afresh, from new angles. Also he was not burdened by that "inveterate tradition according to which thinking takes place remote from perceptual experience."[1] He didn't look and *then* sit down to think, he used his active eyes and mind *together*.

### 1-2/Cards and Discards[4]

Experience using your eyes and mind together in the following puzzle: "In [the] row of five cards shown below, there is only one card correctly printed, there being some mistake in each of the other four. How quickly can you find the mistakes?"

Figure 3.

Another form of thinking in the context of seeing is described by Nobel Laureate James D. Watson, in *The Double Helix*,[5] a fascinating account of the discovery of the structure of the DNA molecule. Watson and his colleagues visualized this complex structure by interacting directly with a large three-dimensional model. He writes: "Only a little encouragement was needed to get the final soldering accomplished in the next couple of hours. The brightly shining metal plates were then immediately used to make a model in which for the first time all the DNA components were present. In about an hour I had arranged the atoms in positions which satisfied both the x-ray data and the laws of stereochemistry. The resulting helix was right-handed with the two chains running in opposite directions.

> ...Another fifteen minutes' fiddling by Francis [Crick] failed to find anything wrong, though for brief intervals my stomach felt uneasy when I saw him frowning."

Although a complex structure such as the DNA molecule is difficult to visualize in imagination or on paper, one of Watson's colleagues scorned the model shown in Figure 4. However, Watson observed that his Nobel prize-winning success by this method of visual thinking convinced the doubter "that our past hooting

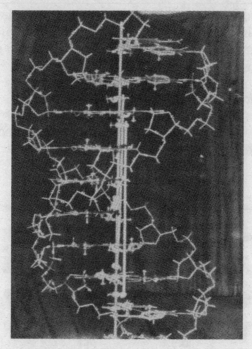

Figure 4.

about model-building represented a serious approach to science, not the easy
resort of slackers who wanted to avoid the hard work necessitated by an honest
scientific career."

Watson's account in *The Double Helix* also gives the reader excellent
insight into the competitive excitement of science. Ideally, the next problem (an
experience in thinking in the direct context of seeing) is given in the spirit of a
competition.

### 1-3/Spaghetti Cantilever

With 18 sticks of spaghetti and 24 inches of Scotch tape, construct the longest
cantilever structure that you can. Here are three additional constraints:
1. Tape-fasten the base of the structure within a 6-inch-square horizontal
   area.
2. Don't make drawings. Think directly with the materials.
3. Design and build the structure in 30 minutes.
(Measure length of cantilever from the point on the base nearest to the
overhanging end of the cantilever.)

### Imagining and Thinking

Inner imagery of the mind's eye has played a central role in the thought processes of many creative individuals. In rare thinkers, this inner imagery is extremely clear. For example, Nikola Tesla, the technological genius whose list of inventions includes the fluorescent light and the A-C generator, "could project before his eyes a picture, complete in every detail, of every part of the machine. These pictures were more vivid than any blueprint."[6] Tesla's inner imagery was so like perceptual imagery that he was able to build his complex inventions without drawings. Further, he claimed to be able to test his devices in his mind's eye "by having them run for weeks—after which time he would examine them thoroughly for signs of wear."

Although labels lead us to think of the various sensory modes of imagination as though they occur separately, in actuality imagination is polysensory. Albert Einstein,[7] in a famous letter to Jacques Hadamard, described the important role of polysensory (visual and kinesthetic) imagination in his own extremely abstract thinking: "The words or the language, as they are written and spoken, do not seem to play any role in my mechanism of thought. The psychical entities which seem to serve as elements in thought are certain signs and more or less clear images which can be voluntarily reproduced and combined. ... The above mentioned elements are, in my case, of visual and some of muscular type. Conventional words or other signs have to be sought for laboriously in a secondary stage, when the above mentioned associative play is sufficiently established and can be reproduced at will."

Although Einstein observed that his polysensory imagination could be directed "at will," many important thinkers have obtained imaginative insights more or less spontaneously. For example, the chemist Kekule[8] came upon one of the most important discoveries of organic chemistry, the structure of the benzene ring, in a dream. Having pondered the problem for some time, he turned his chair to the fire and fell asleep: "Again the atoms were gamboling before my eyes.... My mental eye ... could now distinguish larger structures ... all twining and twisting in snakelike motion. But look! What was that? One of the snakes had seized hold of its own tail, and the form whirled mockingly before my eyes. As if by a flash of lightning I awoke." The spontaneous inner image of the snake biting its own tail suggested to Kekulé that organic componds, such as benzene, are not open structures but closed rings.

Those of you who identify high intellectual endeavor exclusively with verbal and mathematical symbols should consider the introspections of Tesla, Einstein, and Kekulé with special care. Has something been overlooked in your education? The following problem, for example, is best solved by inner imagery. Has your education prepared you for this kind of problem-solving?

### 1-4/Painted Cube

Shut your eyes. Think of a wooden cube such as a child's block. It is painted. Now imagine that you take two parallel and vertical cuts through the cube, dividing it into equal thirds. Now take two additional vertical cuts, at 90° to the first ones, dividing the cube into equal ninths. Finally, take two parallel and horizontal cuts through the cube, dividing it into 27 cubes. Now, how many of these small cubes are painted on three sides? On two sides? On one side? How many cubes are unpainted?

Don't be disappointed if you did poorly on this problem. Mental manipulation of mind's-eye imagery improves with practice.

## Drawing and Thinking

Very few people possess the acuity of mind's eye that enabled Tesla to design and build complex machinery without drawings. Most visual thinkers clarify and develop their thinking with sketches. Watson, recollecting the thinking that preceded his discovery of the DNA structure, writes that one important idea "came while I was drawing the fused rings of adenine on paper."[5] An example of a chemical diagram drawn by Watson is shown in Figure 5. As in Watson's

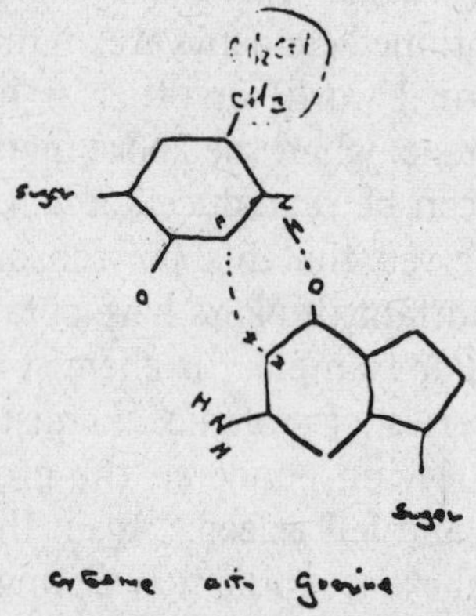

Figure 5.

experience, drawing and thinking are frequently so simultaneous that the graphic image appears almost an organic extension of mental processes. Thus Edward Hill, in *Language of Drawing,*[9] likens drawing to a mirror: "A drawing acts as the reflection of the visual mind. On its surface we can probe, test, and develop the workings of our peculiar vision."

Drawing not only helps to bring vague inner images into focus, it also provides a record of the advancing thought stream. Further, drawing provides a function that memory cannot: the most brilliant imager cannot compare a number of images, side by side in memory, as one can compare a wall of tacked-up idea-sketches.

Two idea-sketches from the notebook of John Houbolt, the engineer who conceived the Lunar Landing Module, are reproduced in Figure 6. Houbolt's drawings show two important attributes of graphic ideation. First, the sketches are relatively "rough." They are not intended to impress or even to communicate; instead, they are a kind of graphic "talking to oneself." Second, one sketch is an abstract schematic of the voyage from earth to moon and back; the other is a relatively more concrete sideview of the landing module. Idea-sketching, like thinking itself, moves fluidly from the abstract to the concrete.

Drawing to extend one's thinking is frequently confused with drawing to communicate a well-formed idea. *Graphic ideation precedes graphic communication;* graphic ideation helps to develop visual ideas *worth communicating.* Because thinking flows quickly, graphic ideation is usually freehand, impressionistic, and rapid. Because communication to others demands clarity, graphic communication is necessarily more formal, explicit, and time-consuming. Education that stresses graphic communication and fails to consider graphic ideation can unwittingly hamper visual thinking.

## Notes

[1]Arnheim, R. "Visual Thinking," in *Education of Vision* (edited by G. Kepes). Braziller.

[2]Feldman, E. *Art as Image and Idea.* Prentice-Hall.

[3]Beveridge, W. *The Art of Scientific Investigation.* Random House (Vintage Books).

[4]Cards and Discards is from *The Book of Modern Puzzles,* by G. L. Kaufman, published by Dover Publications, NY, 1954.

[5]Watson, J. *The Double Helix.* Atheneum.

[6]O'Neil, J. *Prodigal Genius: The Life of Nikola Tesla.* McKay (Tartan Books).

[7]Einstein, A. Quoted by Hadamard, J., in *The Psychology of Invention in the Mathematical Field.* Princeton University Press.

[8]Kekulé, F. von. Quoted by Koestler, A., in *The Act of Creation.* Macmillan.

[9]Hill, E. *The Language of Drawing.* Prentice-Hall (Spectrum Books).

**McKim Comprehension Questions**

1. Is visual thinking possible only in "artistic" professions? Explain.

2. When is drawing, sketching, or doodling most constructive?

3. What are the specific ways in which drawing helps us think?

4. What important discoveries have resulted from visual thinking?

5. What kinds of problems could visual thinking NOT help you with?

**Chapter 5 Practice Session for the Week**

*NOTE:*

1. Use your hand in *all* your reading.
2. Practice at least one hour per day.
3. Set yourself a goal for the week and commit yourself to attaining it. Minimum: *1,000* wpm.

Before beginning your drill, remember to break in your book and practice turning pages for a few minutes.

*DRILL:*

1. Mark off a section of 5,000 words.
2. Preview in 2 minutes, using "S" method. Set up VDI.
3. Read section in 5 minutes maximum. Compute your wpm and circle this number. Add to the VDI.

Repeat this drill in new sections for at least 50 minutes per day for 6 days.

**ANSWERS: Progress Check 1**

1. The direction of your attention.
2. a,d.
3. e.
4. These answers will vary with each person.
5. These answers will vary with each person.
6. Keep in mind your professional/personal reading requirements, the type of material you will concentrate on, and what you plan to do with the material after you have read it.

**ANSWERS: McKim Article**

1. No. Many occupations and activities other than artistic professional require visual thinking.
2. when seeing, imagining and drawing merge into actual interplay.
3. A. it clarifies and develops
   B. it provides a record of the advancing thought stream
   C. it aids memory
   D. it helps to compare images
4. Lunar Landing Module
   Einstein
   Watson, DNA
   Fleming, bacteria
5. problems that require *only* graphic communication.

# ONE WEEK'S PRACTICE RECORD

FROM _____ TO _____
        date              date

| | | | |
|---|---|---|---|
| **1st Session** | Highest PR:____wpm | Highest R:____wpm | Name of Book:____ _____ |
| total # of mins.____ | Lowest PR:____wpm | Lowest R:____wpm | Comments: |
| **2nd Session** | Highest PR:____wpm | Highest R:____wpm | Name of Book:____ _____ |
| total # of mins.____ | Lowest PR:____wpm | Lowest R:____wpm | Comments: |
| **3rd Session** | Highest PR:____wpm | Highest R:____wpm | Name of Book:____ _____ |
| total # of mins.____ | Lowest PR:____wpm | Lowest R:____wpm | Comments: |
| **4th Session** | Highest PR:____wpm | Highest R:____wpm | Name of Book:____ _____ |
| total # of mins.____ | Lowest PR:____wpm | Lowest R:____wpm | Comments: |
| **5th Session** | Highest PR:____wpm | Highest R:____wpm | Name of Book:____ _____ |
| total # of mins.____ | Lowest PR:____wpm | Lowest R:____wpm | Comments: |
| **6th Session** | Highest PR:____wpm | Highest R:____wpm | Name of Book:____ _____ |
| total # of mins.____ | Lowest PR:____wpm | Lowest R:____wpm | Comments: |
| **7th Session** | Highest PR:____wpm | Highest R:____wpm | Name of Book:____ _____ |
| total # of mins.____ | Lowest PR:____wpm | Lowest R:____wpm | Comments: |
| **8th Session** | Highest PR:____wpm | Highest R:____wpm | Name of Book:____ _____ |
| total # of mins.____ | Lowest PR:____wpm | Lowest R:____wpm | Comments: |

S U M M A R Y

| TOTAL TIME | Highest PR:____wpm Highest Read:____ |
|---|---|
| [ ] | Lowest PR:____wpm Lowest Read:____ |
| | Comments: |

# 6 ——————————— Developing Your Memory

This chapter examines certain points about remembering and gives some procedures to enhance your ability to remember. Effective remembering requires a logical, systematic method of acquiring and storing information. You have begun to apply the study procedure presented in Chapter 4. Now you must be concerned with an information retrieval system to call forth the stored information and use it whenever you desire.

## WHAT IS MEMORY?

It is easy to become confused by the different words associated with the memory process. They are used interchangeably, and also tend to overlap in definition. The various meanings are further diluted because they represent a complex process still not fully understood even by experts in the field of memory.

Comprehending and recalling are separate skills. They develop separately and at different speeds. Therefore, it is possible (and probable, while you are acquiring these new skills) to have good comprehension and, at the same time, poor recall. Be forewarned, then, that simply because you can't remember the material immediately after you have finished reading, this doesn't mean that your comprehension was poor. Remember, comprehension is understanding the material *while* you are reading it. For example, poor results on progress checks in this book may have been due to poor comprehension, but the possibility also exists that your comprehension skills were adequate while your separate recall skills were not.

The disparity between comprehension and recall levels is likely if you consider for a moment that you are making one of the most significant changes in your information processing system since you were in grade school. Your brain is still attempting to cope with the new types and amounts of information input (reading comprehension) and will tend to output (recall) at different times and at different speeds.

If you have practiced diligently, you have given your brain a chance to get used to the larger, more meaningful, and more interesting information flow the study procedure allows. Now it's time to address the issue of output (recall) more directly. The ideal situation is to develop both skills, memory and comprehension, in harmony. This chapter helps you organize your reading and remembering techniques in a way that facilitates high comprehension, without giving recall a chance to drop dramatically.

Implicit in the definition of memory is the assumption that learning has occurred. You cannot remember something you did not initially learn. Thus, memory has the dual meaning of the power of remembering as well as the storage of things learned. There is no object in the brain named memory (although many people have claimed to have lost it), but rather, certain activities give evidence of the existence of an information storehouse—your memory.

To illustrate, we define the various memory activities in the following example. Suppose your memory task is to give a presentation summarizing sales growth in your territory. You don't want to speak exclusively from notes or read your report to those at the meeting. Therefore, you must commit to memory a great deal of the data that you organize and learn. The following is a description of the memory activities you might perform in order to present the material to your staff.

## TYPES OF MEMORY

### Phase One—Registration

Registration is the initial information input process. It includes reading, reflecting, notetaking; i.e., all processes described in Chapter 4. After you have carefully selected from the body of information to which you have access those pertinent points you want to present at the meeting, you then use the study process outlined to learn it.

### Phase Two—Retention

According to I.M.L. Hunter's treatise on memory,* retention is that interval between learning and remembering. It is not an observable phenomena, but rather is inferred from a person's learning and remembering activities. Therefore, we cannot give you a concrete illustration of retention.

### Phase Three—Retrieval

Retrieval is calling forth stored information from your memory banks. If you were to rely solely on your internal stimulus retrieval system, you would

IML Hunter, *Memory*, Pelican Books, 1968, p. 18.

speak without notes at the meeting. This is pure *recall*. On the other hand, speaking with the aid of notes is using an external stimulus to retrieve the information stored in your memory. This is *recognition*.

Recognition is a much easier activity than pure recall. Another example of recognizing would be if you saw a wanted poster in the post office. You may recognize the face as someone you have seen before, but that is the extent of your retrieval. You cannot place where or when or under what circumstances you saw the face. (What are you doing hanging around with those people anyway?) Another aspect of recognition is apparent in this example. You did not supply the initial stimulus to trigger the information retrieval; the poster did. Recognition relies on the external stimulus; therefore it is a more limited, dependent form of remembering.

Recall, on the other hand, is a more difficult retrieval activity because you must supply the initial stimulus. That is why your listening vocabulary (a recognition activity) is usually much larger than your speaking vocabulary (a recalling activity). That is also why your reading vocabulary (a recognition activity) is much larger than your writing vocabulary (a recalling activity). In each recalling activity, speaking or writing, the initial stimulus and information came from your personal storehouse of information. That is also why prior information (prior learning and remembering) is so critical to the quality of your present recalling activities. In your staff meeting, simple recognition of your collected data will be clearly insufficient for your presentation. This chapter discusses methods of improving the much more rigorous, but essential recall process.

Because this book is concerned with saving you time and effort in reading. this chapter is crucial in improving your reading efficiency. No matter how industrious you are in applying your study techniques, no matter how elegant your notes, if you can't remember the material by calling forth pertinent facts and details when needed, then you have wasted your reading time.

## Progress Check 1

1. Memory has the dual definition of: _____

2. Match the word with the correct phrase:

   a. input                          _____ recall

   b. output                         _____ retrieval

   c. no way to measure it           _____ recognition

   d. easiest way to remember        _____ register

   e. hardest way to remember        _____ retain

3. What is the basic distinction between comprehension and remembering?

**Exercises**

Draw a line on the graph on page 152, according to how much information you believe you retain in a given time period. Answers and discussions will follow.

*What the Exercise Tells You.* Assuming that the material is fairly consistent in terms of difficulty, then recall tends *not* to function in exactly the same way as comprehension. If comprehension and recall were consistent, then the line wouldn't dip, but, of course, it does.

Graph 1 illustrates the differences between low recall and the comprehension function and explains why so many people don't recall much after hours of learning. The reason is that recall tends to get progressively worse as time passes, unless the mind is given a brief rest. Consider what happens to recall when you take planned breaks, and remember how the study procedure was constructed in Chapter 4?

The second graph on page 153 illustrates how much learned information seems to evaporate once the learning period ends. If the learned information is not present for you to use after the reading, then you might as well have not read it in the first place.

### SHORT-TERM MEMORY

*Short-Term Memory* is retaining processed information for approximately 24 hours after learning. *Long-Term Memory,* on the other hand, comes into play soon after short-term memory has begun to wane.

Just as recall and comprehension are separate and distinct skills, so too are short term and long-term memory in that you can develop them separately. Just as good recall is highly dependent on good comprehension, long-term memory is dependent on good short-term memory habits. This may sound obvious, but many people make the long-term memory task more difficult by ignoring the aid provided by lodging information in the short-term memory. Don't waste your time relearning material for long-term memory because you didn't take the few minutes after you read the material to firmly install it into your short-term memory.

As noted above, short term memory is the ability to retrieve information soon after the learning process is over. Two interesting situations occur when you graph short-term memory tendencies. First, you retain more of what you learned if a few minutes elapse after the end of the learning period. Second, you lose 80 percent of the information you learned within 24 hours of learning. The

INPUT

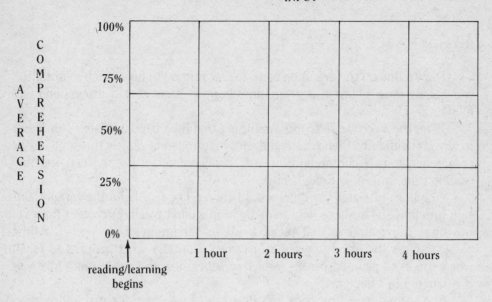

RETRIEVAL

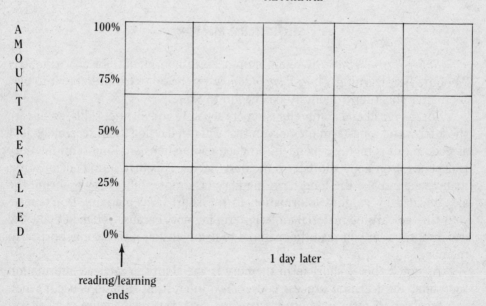

INPUT

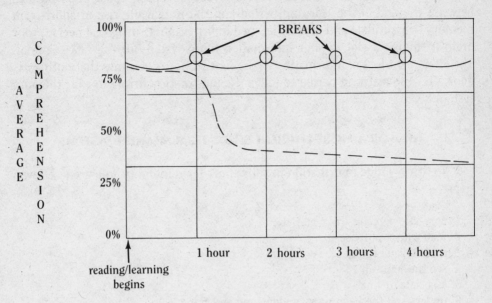

RETRIEVAL

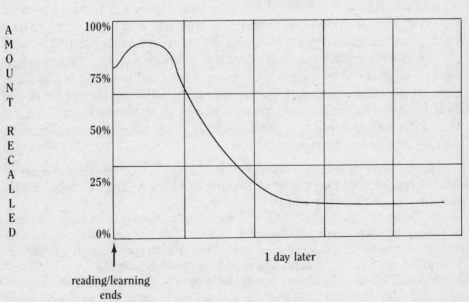

first phenomenon occurs because your brain is taking those few minutes between the end of the learning period and the noticeable rise in short-term memory to assimilate and process learned information. During that period, your brain is finding a slot in your information filing system for the new material. The 80 percent loss of information in the first 24 hours assumes that nothing is done after the learning period to lodge the information firmly in your memory system.

## TIPS FOR A MORE EFFICIENT SHORT-TERM MEMORY SYSTEM

To firmly lodge information in your short-term memory, follow these seven steps:

1. correctly perceive the material
2. read with a purpose
3. involve your ego
4. see the "over-all"
5. associate or link
6. understand the beginning, middle, and end trap
7. do something with it after you are done.

If you find yourself reading long, complicated, unfamiliar passages that do not motivate you to remember them, then your retrieval systems (short-term and long-term memory) will suffer. To enhance your ability to retrieve information easily, develop short-term and long-term memory abilities.

Short-term memory is influenced by conditions and activities before, during, and after the learning period. Some of the conditions can be shaped or modified to benefit your short-term memory. The following tips for improving short-term memory are conditions or activities to better receive, retain, and recall information within that critical first 24 hours after reading, avoiding a dramatic loss of information.

Tip 1: *Correctly Perceive the Material.* Some people have trouble remembering material because they didn't perceive it correctly in the first place. Some reasons material isn't correctly perceived are:

a. *Physical perceptual difficulties.* Some physical disorders can cause people to incorrectly perceive printed material. For instance, they may mistake one word for another or reverse letters when they read. This predicament requires professional assistance before memory practice and improvement will be effective.

b. *Carelessness.* Carelessness is often overlooked as a cause of poor memory. An ineffective memory system could be a symptom of a careless attitude toward reading and remembering. Cursory, disorganized, inaccurate, or inappropriate methods of gathering information will not allow you to recall very well.

c. *Disorganized or poorly written text.* If the material is not presented cogently, your chances of comprehending, much less remembering, are diminished. Many people take all the responsibility for not understanding or remembering material when, in fact, it may be poorly written material. Of course, you can do nothing to alter the author's disorganized presentation, outside of writing a nasty letter; but it is advantageous to be aware that a disorganized text may be at fault. If this is the case, you must design or impose your own organization on the material to understand and remember it.

d. *Reading at an inappropriate speed.* Sometimes you may feel the text is poorly written when, in fact, you are reading the material at an inappropriate speed, usually too slowly. If either the concept or the flow of ideas is indiscernable, speed up and get a different perspective of the material.

*Tip 2: Read with a Purpose.* Reading and remembering are as much processes of selection as they are of comprehension. The information you consciously or accidentally choose to remember must be evaluated according to your general purposes. You needn't read each word on the page with equal consideration because our language doesn't give equal weight to all words. You also needn't give each idea or fact your equal attention for later recall. Any author admits that some information is less important than others in explaining the central theme.

The objection that "everything I read is important" misses the essence of the reading task ... thinking, selecting, rethinking, evaluating, rethinking, and reselecting. The process of eliminating superfluous information begins with the first word you read. Tying yourself to the fruitless task of trying to remember everything you read is not necessary when you have a well-defined purpose. Having such a purpose for reading the material promotes the selection process to its fullest, allowing you to determine what is meaningful and hence useful. To have proper storage and retention of information, the material must have meaning and be useful according to your purpose.

## TYPES OF REMEMBERING

What types of remembering are available to you and what types of remembering will satisfy your purpose for reading? Following are some options in choosing what to remember:

- verbatim memorization of everything
- verbatim memorization of selected portions of the piece
- verbatim memorization to paraphrasing of all general points presented, with attendent facts/details
- recall of general points in your own words exclusively, in the order presented in the text, with one or two substantiating facts or details
- recall in your own words of general or main ideas only. May not be in order presented.
- recall of the general subject of the text and recall of where to find the text to refer to its contents
- know that it exists
- unaware of its existence.

The preceding options have variations and many overlap, but this list shows that you have many more choices for remembering than you might have thought possible.

If you know what you are looking for, you have increased your chances of finding it. Be realistic about the information demands you place on your time and efforts. You can't possibly remember everything, so be selective. Set attainable goals, whatever level they may be. With motivation and diligent practice, you can expand your repertoire of memory skills to suit any reading purpose you desire.

People who feel the most insecure with their reading and remembering usually choose the most comprehensive cloak of security, the first option. Their rationale is that "since I don't know what I want, I'll remember everything and decide later," or "the important points will 'stick' in my memory and the unnecessary points will dissipate." Your brain, however, is not flypaper. If you adopt this attitude, you have assigned yourself a very difficult task. If you feel you need to remember EVERYTHING, stop and evaluate your reading situation in terms of the difficulty of the text, your familiarity with the material, your goals, and your purposes for reading and remembering.

*Establish parameters.* Purposeful reading also sets meaningful parameters around your reading task. Some parameters are physical in that they allow you to see a logical beginning, middle, and end to your reading and remembering task. People who plant themselves in a chair and vow not to get up until they remember "it," have assigned themselves a most difficult job. Remember Graph 1 you filled in at the beginning of the chapter? Remember the drop after approximately 40 minutes of learning? Remember, too, how that curve continues to drop as time passes, unless the brain is allowed a brief rest period to process the input? Your job is always easier when you know its parameters. When you set your purpose before reading, you then know the job's parameters and have made your task much easier.

**Progress Check 2**

1. How long does it take to notice a drop in comprehension while studying? One solution to the drop is:

2. Twenty-four hours after learning, what percentage of information remains?

3. Check those factors that affect whether you correctly perceive the material:

_____a. the book is poorly written or set up

_____b. you are careless

_____c. you are reading at the wrong speed

_____d. you have perceptual difficulties.

4. Set your purpose well because:

     _____a. it gives you meaningful parameters around your learning and remembering task

     _____b. it helps you to see the overall pattern

     _____c. it gives you definition of the task

     _____d. none of the above

     _____e. all of the above.

5. Be selective with your remembering. Why?

*Tip 3: Involve your ego.* Reading with a well-defined purpose also enhances the memory task by providing a reasonable and attainable task in your mind, which is essential to keeping motivation high. People lose motivation quickly if they believe the task is unreasonable or the goal unattainable. So, if you must start small in your remembering task, do so. Find a level of remembering you can achieve with reasonable ease, then set your goals high enough to stretch your skill level; but be sure they are within reason to keep your motivation strong as well.

Motivation, or ego involvement, is vital to remembering. No matter how fastidiously you follow all the other steps outlined in this chapter, if you conclude that you really don't want to remember—you won't. No matter how powerful the external forces are pushing you to remember, if you have analyzed your memory task and decided that you really don't want to remember, stop immediately. You are wasting your time. Better to spend the time analyzing why you don't want to remember than to perform meaningless memory tasks. Weigh the consequences of your not remembering and see if you can create some personal motivation to remember. If you can't come up with some good motivators on your own, you might try the negative motivators of fear or punishment. These tend to be great motivators.

Tip 4: See the Over-All. Seeing the general pattern of the information is critical to organizing the information meaningfully. Hopefully, the author has presented the general concepts logically in the first place, because your task now is to discover that general pattern. Information in most reading selections is usually constructed to show the general theme or basic premise first. Then principal ideas are used to develop the theme or premise.

If you have accurately perceived the incoming information and defined your purpose for reading and remembering, then the next step is to integrate the information into your short-term memory banks.

To perceive the pattern in information implies the ability to effectively move from the specific facts and details of your material to the general ideas or concepts. This is why flexibility in reading speed and technique is an aid to your ability to learn and remember.

If you could sit down and discuss the information with the author, you would probably remember it well because the information would be personalized in a meaningful, direct way. Since that is impossible, you must use other tactics to promote full understanding of the author's message. To remember successfully, adjust the information so it fits your information storehouse. Adjusting the information means first seeing the over-all development of the information.

Most inefficient readers either skip this fundamental step or try to deduce the over-all pattern of ideas from a welter of isolated facts and details. This is a natural mistake for the slow reader because the most apparent thing on the page for the slow reader is words ... words ... words. Objectivity is lost, and a slow reader can't see the forest for the trees using the old, slow, boring method of reading. Reading that way is not only boring, but difficult as well. The difficulty comes from trying to memorize facts and details without first considering the overall pattern of ideas.

The importance of seeing the overall is illustrated by the process most of us use when we look for a street on a map. Assume that your task is to find a small side-street on a map of downtown Manhattan. The map has no index. You can either go block-by-block starting in the upper left-hand corner of the map (as you begin reading a page) looking for your particular street, or you can ask someone what major cross streets are near your street. When you discover the major cross streets, you get a better feel for where the street is, and equally important, *where it is not.* This technique of finding major cross streets is an obvious, simple step to saving time and effort in finding your street.

Searching out the author's main ideas before attending to the various details should be an obvious first step in your reading and remembering task as well. An understanding of the author's main ideas and the order in which they are presented is a tremendous aid to comprehension and retention. Take a few minutes and thoroughly overview the material to be learned and remembered. Those few minutes are well invested.

Tip 5: Associate. All learning and remembering is a process of linking or association. You understand new information in light of previously stored information. You cannot, therefore, learn something if you have no previous information or experience with which to associate it.

For example, a member of a primitive culture who is suddenly thrust into the 20th century is unlikely to understand computers, even though that person might be very "intelligent." The reason is that our hypothetical primative person has no experience base from which an understanding of modern computers can be gained.

*Self-questions*. Since learning (input) and remembering (retrieval) are processes of association, it is helpful to understand how this association process works. When reading, it is also critical to understand that you are actively participating in a process of association. This requires that you spend time thinking and reflecting during your reading periods. An example of reflective thinking is engaging in self-questioning. Ask questions such as, "What is this person trying to say?" "Does this have any relationship to what I already know about this subject?" and "If so, how does it relate to what I already know?" Engage in self-questioning at the end of a separate unit of information, the information contained under a chapter subheading, at the end of a complete chapter, or at the end of a one-issue report. The point is, before you move on to a new series of issues, further enhance your short-term memory processes by self-questioning. It is one method of reinforcing the association process.

*Put it in your own words to personalize it*. Another activity to help make more effective associations is to translate the information into your own words. Most of the information stored in your memory that you remember with any ease has been translated into your own words, ranging from your memories of childhood to the complicated problems of your professional life. You have made this information yours by couching it in terms that are meaningful and important to you. Help your effort to read and remember with ease by doing the same thing with new information you want to remember.

Now that you have associated the new information with previously learned material and have also used your own words to store it, you can use linking or association to retrieve the information. If you can't call forth the exact information you need immediately, it is possible to use association to work toward your desired information. Rather than becoming frustrated because you cannot recall the required information, use whatever you *can* recall to pull what else you need from your memory banks. Consider the information you do have as an opportunity to discover the information you need. A positive attitude plays an important role in whether you can use this technique effectively.

Remember that the VDI's introduced in Chapter 4 were structured to take advantage of the association process. The VDI can also accommodate information that does not come out of your memory banks in precisely the order that you sometimes desire. Information is sometimes retrieved out of input order. This should not be a hindrance if you use the VDI. The VDI is structured to allow you to find the links to any piece of information you desire, regardless of the order of input or output.

**Progress Check 3**

1. Name three external motivators that help to get the remembering task done.

2. Why is seeing the overall hard for slow readers?

3. Flexibility in speed and technique will allow you to move back and forth, from specific to general. The ability to move from specific facts/details to the general ideas/concepts relies upon your _____.

4. Identify which of the following ways that you can use association to remember material.

_____a. self-questioning

_____b. make a VDI

_____c. compare with previous information

_____d. put the information into your own words.

Tip 6: Beginning, Middle and End Trap. When you are working at the task of reading and remembering, you will find that sometimes there are gaps in your learning and remembering. Some of these information gaps are caused by a lag in concentration, while others are caused by a sudden rise in the difficulty of the material. Another reason for remembering gaps relates to your brain—how it processes and remembers information, and in what order the brain retrieves that information. For most learners, when they have a considerable amount of material to read and remember, the beginning, middle and end of the material are not remembered in the consecutive order, or with equal ease.

Most people tend to forget the middle piece of information *first*, then the beginning, and finally the end. If you simply are aware of this phenomena, then you can guard against this tendency to drop the middle by intensifying your efforts during the middle portion of your reading or by beginning your review sessions with special attention to the middle portion. This is also true of information supplied during business meetings, classroom lectures, and conversations. Furthermore, it may be necessary to do something special for emphasis if the entire piece of information is to stay lodged in your memory. Special emphasis can be achieved by creative notetaking or mnemonic devices.

Tip 7: Do Something with It. To retain information in your short-term memory banks, actively reinforce it. Reinforcement counteracts "immediate forgetting." (Refer to Graph 1 at the beginning of the chapter.)

"Immediate forgetting" can be described as follows. When your brain receives any item to be remembered, it puts into action a complex series of events. Words perceived set up chemical reactions in your optic nerve and send electrical impulses to your brain, which, in turn, give rise to patterns of activity in your brain. The activity persists briefly, then is extinguished or supplanted by new activity patterns. This decreasing of brain activity is responsible for immediate forgetting. If you do not want the information to be lost, you must selectively maintain and reinforce those pieces of information you want to retain by doing something with them after you have read.

*Do nothing.* Once you have finished reading material, you have several options as to what to do with it: write about it, talk about it, think about it, or close the book, close your mouth, and close your mind. If you chose not to do something with the material after reading it, you have diminished your chances of the information staying in your short-term memory.

*Think about it.* Once you have eliminated the option of doing nothing with the material, you are left with three other options. Thinking about the material after you are finished is the easiest, but least effective activity. It is very easy to delude yourself into believing that you remember the material with a passive thinking session after reading. Do not be confused with the reflection that should take place during any reading session. Passive thinking is not truly fulfilling the requirement to "do something with it" *after* you finish reading. You are usually much too lenient with yourself when it comes to a serious test of your learning and memory.

*Talk about it.* Sometimes talking to someone after reading something helps improve your chances of remembering it. This type of post-reading activity may not always be practical, but it can help you test yourself as to whether you have grasped the main points and supportive data in the material as well as identify any information gaps. Any time you can place the information in more than one context, e.g., from the visual context of reading to the speaking and hearing context, the better your chances of remembering. The drawback is that the "victim" of your memory technique may or may not be in a position to give you proper feedback as to the validity of your recall of the material. Also, your words as you speak them are quite transient and may not indicate your ability for long-term recall. Thus, talking about the information does not provide a permanent record for later review and does not illustrate the particular pattern that could be unfolding for you visually on paper.

The more you go over the post-reading activity and the more vivid the associations, the better your chances will be for remembering. For example, anyone who was old enough to remember the day President John Kennedy was assassinated can talk with great clarity about many national and personal details associated with that day. You may remember what you had for lunch, who was with you, what you were wearing—seemingly minor details that even now you can call forth. You will remember that tragic day better than many other happier days, because the vividness of those events cause you to associate them with other, apparently minor details.

*Write about it.* The post-reading activity that allows for the most vivid representation of your reading is to design a VDI. Sometimes the material lends its own vitality to making your notes interesting and vivid, such as in the Kennedy example above. Other times, however, you have to be creative in your design of a VDI in order to remember effectively.

Writing about the material should NOT be a verbatim rewrite from the text for 99 percent of the notes you take. Sometimes a direct quote is essential, but then you should be prepared to memorize and repeat that quote in later self-testing. If you find you don't need to memorize the quote, then put it into your notes in your own words. Your notes should also be brief. Don't rewrite the book. An overwhelming desire to rewrite the book reflects insecurity with the material. You may need to study the material differently. Check the list of study possibilities in Chapter 4. If you still want to rewrite the book, put it into your own words and see that you get paid for it.

Creating a VDI reinforces the information for your memory system by repetition, as well by placing the information into a different context (your own words) and onto another paper. Creating a VDI can show you where you might have information gaps and also gives a personal, permanent record of the material that you read. If your VDI is good, it becomes more important to you than the original text. Consequently, making a VDI is the most effective post-reading activity you can perform.

**Progress Check 4**

1. The beginning, middle and end trap says:

you forget the _____ FIRST

you forget the _____ LAST

2. How can you overcome the beginning, middle, end traps?


3. "Do something with" it is another term for _____ that combats immediate forgetting.

4. Which of the above options is the least effective for remembering?

5. Which of the above options is the most effective for remembering?

## LONG-TERM MEMORY: REVIEW IS THE KEY

If you have decided your purpose for reading is to recall information much later, then you must lodge the information into your long-term memory system.

The element of time now becomes important in order to call forth the appropriate information. As you add to your memory store-house, bits and pieces of information may be reshuffled, replaced, or reorganized in light of the new information's importance or volume. The further in time from the original learning experience, the greater the probability that the information will be "misplaced" or "lost" in your brain's "filing system" because time tends to deteriorate the information unless you have an effective storage and retrieval system.

The key to successfully remembering a substantial body of difficult information after a long period of time is periodic, effective review.

### Review Is Not Mindless Repetition

You must understand the distinction between review and repetition. Repeating the information over and over in your head will not insure that you will remember. Good reviewing involves some repetition, but the most important aspect of the review is actively thinking about the material again and in different contexts. One way to artificially create different contexts is to revise your notes. Another way to get a different perspective on the material is to change the chronological order in which it was presented. For example, you may begin a review session by looking at the middle portion of your notes first.

Another very important activity to help insure that long-term memory is effective is to view and think about the old information in light of new, subsequent information. Do the old and new pieces of information relate? How? Thinking about the relationships between new and old information is one of the easiest, most pleasant methods of enhancing long-term memory. If you have fulfilled the requirements for improving your short-term memory, you have come a long way toward promoting your long-term memory as well. All you need now is a programmed pattern of review, the mortar that sets the information firmly in your mind for as long as you desire.

### When to Review

The first step to establishing a programmed pattern of review is to know the particular times when recall tends to drop. Refer to the charts at the beginning of the chapter and identify the time sequences common to most learners. Extensive experimentation, as represented by the charts on pages 152-53, tends to confirm when those critical times of information loss occur. Knowing when those critical times occur, tells you exactly when you need to review. This can save you time because it prevents you from reviewing information when you don't really need to. It can save you effort because it can warn you that you have passed an important review stage and will have to be especially diligent during your next review session.

## FOUR STAGES OF REVIEW

### First Review Session

This session should occur 10 minutes after a 50-minute learning period (using the study procedure). The session itself should take around 10 minutes and will serve to hold the information until the second information loss time.

### Second Review Session

This session occurs 24 hours after the first learning period and should take 2-4 minutes. This will hold the information until the third information loss time.

### Third Review Session

This session should occur approximately one week after the initial learning session and should take 2-4 minutes. This will hold the information until the fourth information loss time.

### Fourth Review Session

This last session occurs approximately one month after the initial learning session and should take 2-4 minutes. After the final session, depending on your information needs and how many times you call forth this information, you will be able to recall the information whenever you want.

## NATURE OF THE REVIEW SESSION

The review sessions should be intensive, concentrated efforts to remember according to your needs. The first review session should be the most rigorous and should include a revision of your VDI that visually redesigns the information in the most personally meaningful way. This may include emphasis in problem areas, reorganization of the main ideas into different order, and/or association with previous information. In the first session, keep the laws of the beginning, middle, and end trap in mind as you review. The more contexts and perspectives you can view your information from, the better chance you have of remembering it. Use your key words in the margins to move from the general to the specific and back again. You should also construct VDI's from memory, and test yourself without notes if your purpose is to recall without external stimuli—a rigorous, but fruitful method of review.

Review sessions 2, 3, and 4 should also be concentrated efforts at thinking about and remembering the material. You may not need to totally revise your notes, but additional comments and points could be added in light of new information. Testing yourself by creating new VDI's is very effective for the short 2–4 minute sessions. Also, using key words to bring forth the details and supportive data may be useful in these latter sessions. Looking at your fact and detail side of the VDI sheet requires you to visualize the progression of ideas in the material. Check all new VDI's that you create in these review sessions with your original notes. Don't revise incorrect information, but do look for new insights into the original material. Watch how the information shifts and changes, grows or disappears, according to your growth as an efficient reader/learner.

**Progress Check 5**

Match each word with its definition:

1. memory
2. short-term memory
3. register
4. retain
5. recognize
6. recall
7. experience base

a. the most rigorous type of memory
b. the easiest type of memory retrieval
c. your memory system
d. the sum of your knowledge that you use for learning and remembering
e. the power of remembering and that which is stored
f. the unknown phase in your memory system
g. information retrieval in the first 24 hours
h. input of information

---

**Reading Selection**

Read the following selection at a minimum of 750 words per minute. Your purpose is to discover the main ideas and to read at the minimum speed.

1) find the key words to see the over-all
2) put the main ideas into your own words
3) associate the main ideas with information in your personal memory system
4) which main ideas will you tend to forget first?

# What Is Technical Writing?

W. Earl Britton

Professor Britton classifies the major definitions of technical writing, then elaborates on the definition that he finds most acceptable. Although the selection is written for teachers, it should pose little difficulty for the student reader.

Although the dean of an engineering college once denied the very existence of technical writing, many of us are confident of its reality. But we are not sure that we can convince others of its uniqueness. This uncertainty deepens when we observe the variety of activities incorporated under this label, as well as those that barely elude its scope. Our schools do little to clarify the situation with such course titles as technical writing, engineering writing, engineering English, scientific English, scientific communications, and report writing. Nor do the national societies help with their emphasis upon medical writing, biological writing, science writing, and business English. Applying the general term *technical writing* to a field of such diversified activities is convenient but misleading, yet this is the current practice. In view of the confusion, there is little wonder that a teacher in this field should often be asked, even by colleagues, "What is this technical writing you teach, and how does it differ from any other?"

In addition to satisfying this query, a truly helpful definition should go much further and illuminate the tasks of both the teachers and authors of technical writing. This requirement has been fulfilled in varying degrees by a number of definitions already advanced, the most significant of which form four categories.

Technical writing is most commonly defined by its subject matter. Blickle and Passe say:

> Any attempt ... to define technical writing is complicated by the recognition that exposition is often creative. Because technical writing often employs some of the devices of imaginative writing, a broad definition is necessary. Defined broadly, technical writing is that writing which deals with subject matter in science, engineering, and business.[1]

Mills and Walter likewise note that technical writing is "concerned with technical subject matter," but admit the difficulty of saying precisely what a

W. Earl Britton, "What Is Technical Writing," *College Composition and Communication,* May 1965, pp. 113-116.

technical subject is. For their own purpose in writing a textbook, they call a technical subject one that falls within science and engineering. They elaborate their view by adding four large characteristics of the form: namely, its concern with scientific and technical matters, its use of a scientific vocabulary and conventional report forms, its commitment to objectivity and accuracy, and the complexity of its task, involving descriptions, classifications, and even more intricate problems.[2]

The second approach is linguistic, as illustrated in an article by Robert Hays, who, admitting the existence of technical writing without actually defining it, remarks upon its conservativeness, its Teutonic subject-verb-object word order, and the fact that it shares with other forms of writing the "common" English vocabulary. However, he cites two fundamental differences between technical and other prose. The psychological difference is the writer's "attitude of utter seriousness" toward his subject, and his dedication to facts and strict objectivity. But the greater difference, at least for "teachers and students of technical writing, is linguistic," in that technical style demands a "specialized vocabulary, especially in its adjectives and nouns."[3]

The third definition concentrates on the type of throught process involved. This approach underlies some of the research being directed by A. J. Kirkman, of the Welsh College of Advanced Technology in Cardiff, who has been investigating the causes of unsatisfactory scientific and technical writing. His group is examining in particular the suggestion that a distinction exists between ways of thinking and writing about literary and scientific subjects. The theory postulates two types of thinking, each with its own mode of expression. Associative thought belongs to history, literature, and the arts. Statements are linked together by connectives like *then* and *rather*, indicating chronological, spatial, or emotional relationships. Sequential thought belongs to mathematics and science. Statements are connected by words like *because* and *therefore*, revealing a tightly logical sequence. Professor Kirkman suggests that the weakness of much scientific writing results from forcing upon scientific material the mode of expression appropriate to the arts. He adds:

> The important distinction is that sequential contexts call for comparatively inflexible lines of thought and rigid, impersonal forms of expression, whereas associative contexts permit random and diverse patterns of thought which can be variously expressed.[4]

Finally, technical writing is sometimes defined by its purpose. This approach rests upon the familiar differentiation between imaginative and expository prose, between DeQuincey's literature of power and literature of knowledge. Brooks and Warren find the primary advantage of the scientific statement to be that of "absolute precision." They contend that literature in general also represents a "specialization of language for the purpose of precision" but add that it "aims at treating kinds of material different from those of science," particulary attitudes, feelings, and interpretations.[5]

Reginald Kapp pursues a similar line by dividing writing into imaginative and functional literature. Imaginative literature involves personal response and is evocative, functional literature concerns the outer world that all can see. Functional English, he says, presents "all kinds of facts, of inferences, arguments, ideas, lines of reasoning. Their essential feature is that they are new to the person addressed." If imaginative literature attempts to control men's souls, functional English should control their minds. As he writes, the technical and scientific author "confers on the words the power to make those who read think as he wills it."[6]

All of these approaches are signficant and useful. Kirkman's suggestions are certainly intriguing, but I find Kapp's classification particularly helpful and want to extend it slightly.

I should like to propose that the primary, though certainly not the sole, characteristic of technical and scientific writing lies in the effort of the author to convey one meaning and only one meaning in what he says. That one meaning must be sharp, clear, precise. And the reader must be given no choice of meanings; he must not be allowed to interpret a passage in any way but that intended by the writer. Insofar as the reader may derive more than one meaning from a passage, technical writing is bad; insofar as he can derive only one meaning from the writing, it is good.

Imaginative writing—and I choose it because it offers the sharpest contrast—can be just the opposite. There is no necessity that a poem or play convey identical meaings to all readers, although it may. Nor need a poem or play have multiple meanings. The fact remains, nevertheless, that a work of literature may mean different things to different readers, even at different times. Flaubert's *Madame Bovary* has been interpreted by some as an attack on romanticism, and in just the opposite way by others who read it as an attack on realism. Yet no one seems to think the less of the novel. Makers of the recent film of *Tom Jones* saw in the novel a bedroom farce, whereas serious students of Fielding have always regarded it as an effort to render goodness attractive. Varied interpretations of a work of literature may add to its universality, whereas more than one interpretation of a piece of scientific and technical writing would render it useless.

When we enter the world of pure symbol, the difference between the two kinds of communication—scientific and aesthetic—becomes more pronounced. Technical and scientific writing can be likened to a bugle call, imaginative literature to a symphony. The bugle call conveys a precise message: get up, come to mess, retire. And all for whom it is blown derive identical meanings. It can mean only what was intended. But a symphony, whatever the intention of the composer, will mean different things to different listeners, at different times, and especially as directed by different conductors. A precise meaning is essential and indispensable in a bugle call; it is not necessarily even desirable in a symphony.

The analogy can be extended. Even though the bugle call is a precise communication, it can be sounded in a variety of styles. An able musician can play taps with such feeling as to induce tears, and it is conceivable that a magician might blow reveille so as to awaken us in a spirit of gladness. The fact that scientific writing is designed to convey precisely and economically a single meaning does not require that its style be flat and drab. Even objectivity and detachment can be made attractive.

Because technical writing endeavors to convey just one meaning, its success, unlike that of imaginative literature, is measurable. As far as I am aware, there is no means of determining precisely the effects of a poem or a symphony; but scientific analyses and descriptions, instructions, and accounts of investigations quickly reveal any communication faults by the inability of the reader to comprehend and carry on.

Objection may be raised to this distinction between the two kinds of writing because it makes for such large and broad divisions. This I readily admit, at the same time that I hold this feature to be a decided advantage, in that it removes the difficulty that usually arises when technical writing is defined by its subject matter.

Emphasis upon engineering subject matter in technical writing, for example, has implied that engineering has a monopoly on the form, and that a Ph.D. dissertation in linguistics or even certain kinds of literary criticism and a study of federal economic policy are other kinds of writing. When all such endeavors that convey single meanings are grouped under the label technical and scientific writing, or some other term, for that matter, then division of these into subject areas, instead of creating confusion, becomes meaningful. Some subjects will be far more technological than others, ranging from dietetics to nuclear fission, and in some instances being related to science only by method of approach; some subjects will offer more linguistic difficulty than others; some will require a tighter, more sequential mode of thinking; but all will have in common the essential effort to limit the reader to one interpretation.

It seems to me that this view not only illuminates the nature of technical writing but also emphasizes the kind of training required of our schools. Unfortunately, few educational institutions are meeting the needs in this field. Professor Kirkman mentions the failure of the traditional teachers to provide enough practice in writing on practical subjects. Professor Kapp has insisted that the conventional instruction in formal English courses does not equip a man to teach or practice scientific and technical writing. The Shakespearian scholar, G. B. Harrison, commenting upon his formal writing courses in England, says:

The most effective elementary training I ever received was not from masters at school but in composing daily orders and instructions as staff captain in charge of the administration of seventy-two miscellaneous military units. It is far easier to discuss Hamlet's complexes than to write orders which ensure that five working parties from five different units arrive at the right place at the right time equipped with proper tools for the job. *One learns that the most seemingly simple statement can bear two meanings* and that when instructions are misunderstood the fault usually lies with the wording of the original order.[7] [My italics]

But our strictures should not be confined to the English teachers. All of us in education must share the responsibility for this condition. In fact, I believe that in all too many instances, at least in college, the student writes the wrong thing, for the wrong reason, to the wrong person, who evaluates it on the wrong basis. That is, he writes about a subject he is not thoroughly informed upon, in order to exhibit his knowledge rather than explain something the reader does not understand, and he writes to a professor who already knows more than he does about the matter and who evaluates the paper, not in terms of what he has derived, but in terms of what he thinks the writer knows. In every respect, this is the converse of what happens in professional life, where the writer is the authority; he writes to transmit new or unfamiliar information to someone who does not know but needs to, and who evaluates the paper in terms of what he derives and understands.

B. C. Brookes takes a similar position when he suggests that English teachers concerned with science students should ask them occasionally to explain aspects of their work which they know well so that the teacher who is acquainted with the material will understand it. Such an assignment not only is a real exercise in composition but also taxes the imagination of the student in devising illuminating analogies for effective communication. The teacher's theme should be: "If your paper is not plain and logical to me, then it is not good *science*."[8]

Both Harrison and Brookes recommend the kinds of exercises that are often viewed skeptically at the college level. This is a regrettable attitude, especially since it usually derives from unfamiliarity with the nature and need of such work and from unawareness of its difficulty and challenge. Teachers oriented primarily toward literature see little of interest in this field, but those who enjoy composition—especially its communicative aspect—can find considerable satisfaction here. Of one thing they can always be sure: deep gratitude from those they help.

[1]*Readings for Technical Writers,* ed. Margaret D. Blickle and Martha E. Passe (New York, 1963), p. 3.
[2]Gordon H. Mills and John A. Walter, *Technical Writing* (New York, 1954), pp. 3-5.
[3]Robert Hays, "What Is Technical Writing?" *Word Study,* April 1961, p. 2.
[4]A. J. Kirkman, "The Communication of Technical Thought," *The Chartered Mechanical Engineer,* December, 1963, p. [2].
[5]Cleanth Brooks and Robert Penn Warren, *Understanding Poetry,* 3rd ed. (New York, 1960), pp. 4-5.
[6]Reginald O. Kapp, *The Presentation of Technical Information* (New York, 1957), chaps. I-II.
[7]G. B. Harrison, *Profession of English* (New York, 1962), p. 149.

**Britton Comprehension Questions**

1. What four basic definitions of technical writing does Britton discuss?
2. Which definition does the author prefer? Why?
3. Why does the author discuss the definition in imaginative writing? How does this definition help him in precisely defining technical writing?
4. Scientific analyses, instruction and accounts of investigations are some of the ways that are used to measure one important aspect of technical writing. What is that aspect?
5. What is the appropriate subject matter for technical writing as Britton defines it?

## CONCLUSIONS

Remembering what you read is a skill YOU can acquire and improve with knowledge and practice. The knowledge gives an understanding of the process and a rationale for exchanging your old memory habits for more effective new skills. At first, the steps may seem complicated or cumbersome, just as in the study procedure, but if you apply the memory techniques to the weekly practice session you will see that they are neither. Many students have acquired the remembering skills better and faster with these methods. It takes practice and motivation to become familiar with the techniques. With practice, the skills will become second nature. You won't need to stop and think about what to do next. Once this memory process becomes part of your total learning system, you can concentrate on the content of the material more fully. AFTER you have mastered the entire chapter, you will modify this information according to your needs. Continued use of the memory and other skills learned thus far is the best means of personal validation.

### Chapter 6 Practice Session for the Week

*NOTE:*

1. Use your hand in *all* your reading.
2. Practice at least one hour per day.
3. Set yourself a goal for the week and commit yourself to attaining it. Minimum: *1,000* wpm.

Before beginning your drill, remember to break in your book and practice turning pages for a few minutes.

*DRILL:*

1. Mark off a section of 5,000 words.
2. Preview in 2 minutes using the "S" method. Set up a VDI.
3. Read the section in 5 minutes maximum. Compute your wpm and circle this number. Add to the VDI.

Repeat this drill in new sections for at least 50 minutes per day for 6 days.

### Exercise

1. List the memory requirements you hate to do. List motivators to encourage you to remember them.
2. Why is the VDI so well suited to enhancing short-term and long-term memory?

3. Use the checklist on page 155, "Types of Remembering," to decide which level you need, according to your purposes, for your next reading session at school or work.

## ANSWERS

**Progress Check 1**
  1. dual meaning of the powers of remembering and the storage of things learned.
  2. e,b,d,a,c.
  3. Comprehension means understanding *while* you are reading. Remembering means bringing forth and understanding *after* reading.

**Progress Check 2**

  1. 50 minutes ... take a break every 50 minutes for 10 minutes.
  2. approximately 20 percent.
  3. a,b,c,d.
  4. e.
  5. You cannot remember everything and if you try, you will usually fail.

**Progress Check 3**

  1. fear, reward, punishment.
  2. Because only individual words are apparent.
  3. Flexibility in reading speed.
  4. a,b,c,d.

**Progress Check 4**

  1. the middle first, the end last.
  2. be aware of them and give special emphasis to those selections you will tend to forget.
  3. reinforcement.
  4. think ... talk about the material.
  5. Write.

**Progress Check 5**

  1. e
  2. g
  3. c
  4. f
  5. b
  6. a
  7. d

**ANSWERS: Britton Article**

1. A. Science and engineering.
   B. the writer's attitude of utter seriousness, but more importantly, in a linguistic sense, of a specialized vocabulary.
   C. The type of thought process illustrated by "because and therefore" vs "then and rather," which indicates spatial or emotional relationships.
   D. defined by it's purpose: to be precise.
2. Kapp's, in that the environment of science requires the author's effort for one and only one meaning.
3. because it offers the sharpest contrast.
4. the success of communication.
5. any subject that makes an effort to limit the reader to one interpretation.

# ONE WEEK'S PRACTICE RECORD

FROM _____ TO _____
<br>date           date

1st Session    Highest PR:____wpm Highest R:____wpm Name of Book:____
_____

total # of mins.____    Lowest PR:____wpm Lowest R:____wpm Comments:

2nd Session    Highest PR:____wpm Highest R:____wpm Name of Book:____
_____

total # of mins.____    Lowest PR:____wpm Lowest R:____wpm Comments:

3rd Session    Highest PR:____wpm Highest R:____wpm Name of Book:____
_____

total # of mins.____    Lowest PR:____wpm Lowest R:____wpm Comments:

4th Session    Highest PR:____wpm Highest R:____wpm Name of Book:____
_____

total # of mins.____    Lowest PR:____wpm Lowest R:____wpm Comments:

5th Session    Highest PR:____wpm Highest R:____wpm Name of Book:____
_____

total # of mins.____    Lowest PR:____wpm Lowest R:____wpm Comments:

6th Session    Highest PR:____wpm Highest R:____wpm Name of Book:____
_____

total # of mins.____    Lowest PR:____wpm Lowest R:____wpm Comments:

7th Session    Highest PR:____wpm Highest R:____wpm Name of Book:____
_____

total # of mins.____    Lowest PR:____wpm Lowest R:____wpm Comments:

8th Session    Highest PR:____wpm Highest R:____wpm Name of Book:____
_____

total # of mins.____    Lowest PR:____wpm Lowest R:____wpm Comments:

---

S U M M A R Y

TOTAL TIME

Highest PR:____wpm Highest Read:____

Lowest PR:____wpm Lowest Read:____

Comments:

176

# 7 ══════════════════════════════════ Putting It All Together

## SUMMARY AND FINAL TESTING

You have now completed the basics of the speed reading course. At your disposal are the theory and techniques for fast and more efficient reading in any type of reading material. If you have been diligent in following the course requirements explained in Chapter 1, if you have practiced correctly and regularly, then you are beginning to find these new skills more and more comfortable.

Those of you who were remiss in your practicing may not be as comfortable with all the skills, although your probably can perform them with reasonable ability. If the new skills are to become more comfortable habits, time and persistent use must be considered. You now have all the essential skills necessary to perform any reading task you may encounter, but for the skills to be as comfortable as your old reading habits, you must use them. Remember, the old habits were the product of many years of reinforcement, so give yourself and your new skills a chance with practical application at every opportunity.

Before the final test that will show you your overall progress, look back over the entire course. Many students become somewhat jaded with their speeds and progress as they move through the course because they have focused almost entirely on what lies ahead in their reading tasks. It is useful to look back and see "from whence you have come" in terms of speed and comprehension. Take a moment to review the course goals you set in Chapter 1. Did you meet or exceed those goals? If so, how do you feel about increasing those goals? What have you learned about yourself as a learner and as a student of speed reading? Can any of this information about yourself and how you learn be applied to other learning requirements that you may encounter at work or school?

As stated in Chapter 1, the art of reading is composed of many distinct skills that can be addressed individually, but true reading is the elegant blend of all the skills. Just as rereading in the study process synthesizes the information for you,

177

so should you view this course from a wide perspective. The following is a compilation of the summaries from each chapter in order for you to review the synthesis of your new skills.

Chapter 1 began your course of speed reading by discovering your level of speed and comprehension, setting expectations in terms of just what you needed to invest in the course as well as what you could expect at the end of it.

Chapter 2 explained that the way to read faster and smarter was to acquire a new set of skills that would replace old, inefficient habits. Efficient readers' habits were discussed, along with the habits that promoted those efficient reading skills. The most important factor for more efficient habits was motivation, in that the stronger the motivation, the more quickly and firmly the skills were learned and ingrained. The second most important factor was knowledge or a systematic method to implement the new skills. Knowledge was essential because motivation without knowledge and guidance would have led to frustration. But knowledge could not help you much unless you incorporated these new, more efficient reading skills into your everyday reading requirements. The new skills would turn into comfortable habits through patient and diligent application. Practice was the third factor needed for you to become a successful speed reader.

Chapter 3 began your reading improvement by showing you how to use your hand as a pacer on the page. The old habits that slowed your reading down were directly challenged by the use of your hand, and you noticed the effect of improved reading habits through an increase in speed. Your hand quickly eliminated regressions and other inefficient eye motions. Your span of focus was expanded, subvocalizations were reduced with your Basic Step and "S," and the notion of writing after reading gave your reading time new efficiency and potential. The concept of practice to replace the old habits, plus the proper practice techniques, solidly launched you into faster and smarter reading.

Chapter 4's comprehension skills were initially foremost on your mind, but with practice the steps became readily useful. You were presented with a logical, systematic, flexible method of acquiring information, empowering you with the means for an almost limitless storehouse of knowledge. There was no secret to acquiring it in an efficient, pleasant, and interesting manner. It simply required understanding, motivation, and practice to become a first-rate reader/learner. The skills presented in this chapter were verified by your personal reading experiences. They will stand the test of application and give you a most effective tool if you invest time and effort in polishing the skills.

As discussed in Chapter 5, many people require huge levels of concentration in sporadic reading sessions. As with any skill, concentration can be improved with practice, but you also need to develop the length of your concentration ability. It has been speculated that the average concentration span in a college-level classroom is 17 seconds. That means people who demand hours and hours of high concentration from themselves are unrealistic.

Remember, prepare to concentrate, avoid external distraction, reduce internal distractions, and build your concentration stamina. Extend the time you demand concentration from yourself little by little, until you can expect to direct all of your attention to your material for as long as necessary.

Chapter 6 discussed the differences between remembering and comprehension and stated that better memory is a skill you can improve with knowledge and practice. This chapter gave you an understanding of the process and a rationale for exchanging your old memory habits for new, more effective skills. Just as in the study procedure, the steps may have seemed complicated at first, but you soon discovered that they were not. Many students acquired remembering skills with these methods, but it took practice and motivation to become totally familiar with the techniques. Once the memory techniques became part of your total learning system, you concentrated on the contents of the material more fully and you were able to modify the skills according to your needs. Continued use of the memory and other skills learned thus far is the best means of personal validation.

## READING SELECTION AND FINAL TEST

Use this last selection to determine progress in your skill level. Incorporate any of the skills you have learned in this book to do a good job. The purpose for reading this time is to answer the questions at the end of the selection, while reading as fast as you believe necessary to satisfy your purpose. Remember, to have all the results you desire, you must have practiced the requisite number of hours. If you did not, temper your expectations.

The selection as 2,772 total words. You may wish to break it into smaller sections, read them, and then jot down some notes. Remember to keep track of how much time it took you to read the entire selection.

# Audience Analysis

Thomas Pearsall

Thomas Pearsall, who teaches technical writing at the University of Minnesota, has written several highly respected technical writing textbooks. The selection on audience analysis that is reprinted here is typical of Pearsall's contributions to the study of technical writing. It is one of the most important essays in this text.

### The Audiences in Technical Writing

Probably no other kind of writing matches technical writing in the importance—and, in some ways, the ease—of mating a particular piece of writing to a particular audience. Anyone who has ever picked up a piece of technical writing knows that a report written by an expert for an expert might as well be written in a foreign language, as far as the layman is concerned. Or, conversely, that an expert will become bored by a "popular" article in his field. He may well even be a little condescending toward it. The need for mating audience to report has long been recognized....

But perhaps you have never been told to think about the *purpose of your audience* in reading your paper. Perhaps, to this point, your only audience has been a teacher and his purpose, as far as you could see, was to put red marks on your baby and give it a grade. When you move beyond the classroom, you will have to consider why a reader wants to read your paper and the fund of knowledge he brings to the reading.

You must consider what the reader is going to *do* with the information you give him.

*Is he a laymen?* Then perhaps all he wants to do is read and enjoy your paper and file away a few interesting facts to add to his awareness of the world around him.
*Is he an executive?* He has a profit motive. He may use your paper to make stock-buying decisions or to explore new markets for his company.
*Is he an expert in the subject?* Then he wants new information to add to the large store he already has. Your information may stimulate him to further research or to design a new piece of equipment, or it may help him do a familiar job better.
*Is he a technician?* He wants information that will help him understand and maintain the equipment the engineer or scientist has given him to work with.
*Is he an operator of equipment?* Then he wants clear, unequivocal instructions, step by step, in how to get the most out of the equipment he operates.

From Thomas Pearsall, "Audience Analysis," *Audience Analysis for Technical Writing* (Beverly Hills: Glencoe, 1969), pp. ix-xxi.

The true expert on a subject is in an enviable yet difficult position when he sits down to write. He has a mass of information on a specific subject available to him. The difficulty? What to draw from that mass to interest, to inform, to satisfy a particular audience....

As well as understanding his reader's purpose, the writer must understand his reader's knowledge. The writer must know who his reader is, what he already knows, and what he doesn't know. He must know what the reader will understand without background and without definitions. He must know what information he must elaborate, perhaps with simple analogies. He must know when he can use a specialized word or term and when he cannot. He must know when and how to define specialized words that he can't avoid using. All this is asking a great deal of the writer. But the good writer knows that each particular reader brings his experience *and his experience only* to his reading. Not to understand this is to miss the whole point of writing.

To be a good writer you must know your audience—its purpose and its knowledge.

## A Caution

Before I elaborate about the five audiences, let me caution you. No audience is uniform and classified simply into a neat category. I speak of a lay audience, or an executive audience, but these audiences are by no means totally homogeneous units. An audience is much more analogous to an aggregate of hard, sharp, different-sized rocks than it is to a mass of smooth marble.

There are laymen and there are laymen. A physicist reading a paper on biology is something of a layman because he is out of his specialty. Yet because he understands the scientific process he is much less of a layman than a musician reading the same paper. There are executives who deal only in market research. There are executives who are personnel experts. The first is interested in a new piece of equipment because it may open up a new market. The second is interested in the same piece of equipment because it may change the way he staffs a plant.

Even at the operator level you will not find a comfortable, single audience. Here the educational level may vary tremendously. The operator may be a high school dropout trained to run a lathe and little else. Or he may be an astronaut with an M.S. in mechanical engineering who must be shown how to operate a hand-held maneuvering unit while deep in space.

Take my generalizations and narrow them as much as possible to fit the individuals you are dealing with. Fortunately, in technical writing this can often be done fairly precisely.

I speak of writing for *the executive*, thinking of the term as representing *most* executives. Someday you may be writing for *one* executive. Get to know him. Talk with him. Find out his education, his job experience. If you work at it you can know his background as well as you know your own....

## The Layman

Who is the layman? He is the fourth-grade boy reading a simplified explanation of atomic fission in terms of mouse traps and ping pong balls. He is the bank clerk reading a Sunday newspaper supplement story about desalination. He is the biologist with a Ph.D. reading an article in *Scientific American* entitled "The Nature of Metals." In short, the layman is everyman (and every woman) once he is outside his own particular field of specialization.

We can make only a few generalizations about him. He is reading for interest. He is reading to tune in more accurately on the universe. He is not very expert in the field (or else he would not be reading a layman's article). Probably, his major interest is practical. He is much more concerned with what things do than in how they work. He is more interested in how computers will affect his daily life than in the fact that they work on a binary number system. He is probably more attuned to fiction and television than scientific exposition. He likes drama. For this reason the use of narration, when possible, is often an effective device when writing for the layman. Relate anecdotes and incidents to illustrate what something is and what it does.

Beyond these few simple statements the layman presents a bewildering complexity of interests, skills, educational levels, and prejudices. How then can we define exactly how to write for him? The truth is that we cannot—completely. But we can make some general statements about his needs, interests, likes, and dislikes that—to paraphrase Lincoln—apply to all of the laymen some of the time, some of the laymen all of the time, but not to all of the laymen all of the time.

To simplify matters a little, let's get a picture in our minds of what might be an average layman: He is an individual fairly bright and interested in science and technology. He has at least a high school education. He reads fairly well, and he has a smattering of mathematics and science, but he is a little vague about both subjects. How do we treat him? What approaches are best when we write for him?

## Background

To begin with, the layman needs to be given background material in the subject. We must assume he knows little or nothing about the specialty. An AEC booklet entitled *Atomic Energy in Use* is a simplified layman's explanation of how a nuclear reactor works. Chapter I gives a history of uranium, and Chapter II explains nuclear radiation. The beginning of Chapter II is instructive in how to give a layman background information. It begins:

Light is radiation that we can see. Heat is radiation that we can feel. Radio and television waves and X-rays are electromagnetic waves of radiation that we can neither see nor feel, but with whose usefulness we are well acquainted.

Now we are hearing more and more about another kind of radiation as a result of man's continuing scientific and engineering achievements.

This is nuclear radiation.

Nuclear radiation consists of a stream of fast-flying particles or waves originating in and coming from the nucleus, or heart, of an atom. It is a form of energy we have come to call atomic, or nuclear energy.[1]

The author begins with the familiar—light radiation and heat radiation. There is no pretense that the reader knows all about light and heat radiation; that he could, for example, construct mathematical models of such phenomena in the way a physicist could. Nor does the writer attempt to give the reader such complicated theory. The writer knows that the average layman dimly understands that light, heat, and electromagnetic waves are forms of energy that somehow travel from point A to point B and can therefore be *used* in various practical ways. Nuclear radiation is a similar form of radiation and that's the only point the writer wants immediately to make.

To make his point the writer has relied upon analogy—comparing the unfamiliar to the familiar. There is no better device to help the lay reader. In the everyday world around us—in light bulbs, radios, garden hoses, faucets, windows, mirrors, trees, tennis rackets, baseballs, hot air registers, clay, loam, granite, ocean waves—are countless things known and somewhat understood by the layman that the writer can use to explain about every law of science. It's a question of imagination and of being willing to talk in lay terms without being condescending.

Give the layman, then, a grounding in your subject using familiar things as points of comparison.

### Definitions

Laymen need specialized words and terms defined. There are at least two reasons why you shouldn't force a reader to go to the dictionary while he is reading your work.

First, you are the host. You have invited your reader to come to you. You owe him every courtesy and defining difficult terms is a courtesy. Remember that the layman reads primarily for interest. If you force him to the dictionary every fourth line, his interest will soon flag.

Second, if you give the definition, you can limit or expand the term in the way that is most useful to you. In Chapter II of *Atomic Energy in Use* the author's emphasis in the second half of the chapter is upon radiation control and radiation safety. His definition of an alpha particle reflects that emphasis: "Alpha particles are comparatively heavy particles given off by the nuclei of heavy radioactive materials such as uranium, thorium, and radium. They can travel about an inch in air and can readily be stopped by the skin or by a thin sheet of paper."[2]

If the writer had left the reader to look up the word himself, the emphasis wanted would have been lost. Compare this definition from *Webster's Seventh New Collegiate Dictionary* and you'll see the difference: "Alpha particle: a positively charged nuclear particle identical with the nucleus of a helium atom that consists of 2 protons and 2 neutrons and is ejected at high speed in certain radioactive transformations." Nothing is said about the relative ease with which alpha particles can be blocked, a fact important to the writer's later emphasis on radiation control.

Define terms, then, both for courtesy and understanding and to aid your own exposition.

### Simplicity

There are several ways to keep an article simple for the layman. Two of them I have already discussed: give him needed background in a way he can understand and define those specialized terms that you must use. Most often, avoid specialized words for which you can find simple substitutes. The expert can read certain meanings into the word *homeostasis* and you should use it for him, but for the layman *stable state* or *equilibrium* will serve as well. But, another caution here. Most laymen like to enrich their vocabulary. So, don't avoid technical terms altogether. Just don't put them together in incomprehensible strings with a "reader-be-damned" attitude.

Some scientific specialities are loaded with mathematics. Others, such as biochemistry, are full of formulas and complicated charts and diagrams incomprehensible to the layman. Mathematics, formulas, and diagrams are useful shorthand expressions for the expert. He knows he can attain a precision with them that he can attain in no other way. But what the expert sometimes forgets is that he has spent years learning how to handle such precise tools. The layman, however, most likely cannot handle them. He either has had no training in them beyond high school, or he learned them so long ago that he has forgotten them.

### Conclusion

The layman is the hardest audience to write for because he is so difficult to pin down and define. We can generalize that for him we should provide ample background—without mathematics or complicated formulas—definitions, photographs and simple charts. Remember, he is reading mainly for interest and his interest is mainly practical: What effect will this sicentific development have on me? Your cardinal rules in writing for the layman are to keep things uncomplicated, interesting, practical, and, if possible, a touch dramatic.

## The Executive

Much of what I said about the layman applies directly to the executive. You cannot assume that he possesses very much knowledge in the field you are writing about. While most executives have college degrees and many have technical experience, they represent many disciplines, and not necessarily the one you are writing about. Some may have little technical background but have been trained in management, psychology, social science, or the humanities.

Like the layman, the executive's chief concern is with practical matters. He is more concerned with what things do rather than in how they work. He wants to know what effects a technological development will bring. He needs simple background. However, he can probably handle and wants a bit more technical background than does the layman. James W. Souther, who has made an extensive study of the executive and his needs, suggests that writing for him be approximately on the level found in *Scientific American*.[3] The executive will want most purely technical terms defined for him. You should avoid shop jargon when addressing him. He is a busy man; don't force him to a dictionary any more than you would the layman.

When writing for the executive, write in plain language, using sentences averaging about 21 words. Avoid mathematics. Use simple graphs of the layman type: bar graphs, pie charts, and pictographs.

But while the executive resembles the lay reader in many ways, there is a significant difference. The layman reads primarily for interest. The executive is interested, too, but he has a much more vital concern. As an executive *he must make decisions based upon what he reads*. And his decisions revolve around two poles: *profits and people.* How much money will a technological development cost? What new markets will it open? How much money will a technological development make? Does the development call for restaffing a plant? Will new people have to be hired or old people retrained? There are many other ramifications in the executive's decision-making process, but people and profits are the two poles about which all decisions revolve.

## The Executive's Needs

What is the executive interested in? What questions does he want you to answer in a report written for him?

He wants to know how a new process or piece of equipment can be used. What new markets will they open up? What will they cost, and why is the cost justified? What are the alternatives?

Why was your final choice chosen over the other alternatives? Give some information about the also-rans. Convince the executive that you have explored the problem thoroughly. For all the alternatives include comments on cost, size of the project, time to completion, future costs in upkeep and replacement, and the effects on productivity, efficiency, and profits. Consider such things as new staffing, competition, experimental results, troubles to be expected. What are the risks involved?

Be honest. Remember that if your ideas are bought, they are *your* ideas. Your reputation will stand or fall on their success. Therefore, don't overstate your case. Qualify your statements where necessary.

Give your conclusions and recommendations clearly. In writing any report for the executive, remember that you must interpret your material and present its implications, not merely give the facts. Souther points out that "the manager seldom uses the detail, though he often wants it available. It is the *professional judgment* of the writer that the manager wants to tap."[4] ...

## The Expert

To many laymen, writing meant for the expert seems incredibly dull. But to the expert nothing could be more exciting. In the well-written report in his specialty, he has facts to chew—the expert is a man in love with facts. He also has inferences drawn from those facts to hail as new and true or to dispute as examples of faulty reasoning. He is akin to the symphony conductor who can read a score and *hear it* and judge its potential. The layman, like the musical audience, must wait for the interpretation by the conductor and his full orchestra before he can appreciate the same score.

Who is the expert? For our purposes I will define him as a scientist or engineer with either an M.S. or a Ph.D. in his field or a B.S. and years of experience. He may be a college professor, an industrial researcher, or an engineer who designs and builds. Whichever of these he is, he knows his field intimately. When he reads he seldom looks for background information. Rather, he is looking for a new body of information, new conclusions, or perhaps new and better techniques to help him in his work....

## The Technician

The technician is the man at the heart of any operation. He is the man who finally brings the scientist's imaginative research and the engineer's calculations and drawings to life. He builds equipment and after it is built he maintains it. He is an intensely practical man, perhaps with years of experience behind him. He is the one who can say, "you know, sir, if we used a wing nut here, instead of a hexagonal, the operator would have a lot easier job getting that plate on and off," and he'll be right. He's a man well worth listening to and certainly he is a man for whom you should write well.

The technician's educational level varies. Most typically he will range anywhere from a high school graduate to a junior engineer with a B.S. The high school graduate will probably have a great deal of on-the-job training and experience. The junior engineer may be better trained in theory but have less practical experience. The technician has limitations. He most likely will not be able to follow complicated mathematics and he'll grow restive with too much theory. Also you will want to take care with your sentence length when writing for the technician. Research cited by Rudolf Flesch indicates that sentences over 17 words long can be classified as difficult.[5] Other research indicates that high school students write sentences 17 to 19 words long.[6] Unless you are sure that your technicians are college trained, give them sentences that they are used to and can handle—about 17 words or less on the average.

## The Operator

In many ways, the operator is a cross between the layman and the technician. Like the technician, he works with technical equipment, operating it and sometimes performing simple maintenance on it. Like the layman, he may have little real technical and scientific knowledge. Also, like laymen, operators may come from many educational levels. For example, some of the divers in undersea exploration are Naval petty officers with a high school education. Others are oceanographers with Ph.D.'s. Both groups need equally simple instructions in how to operate Naval diving equipment.

Because of the similarities between operators, technicians, and laymen, much of what I have said already applies in this section as well. I will here merely attempt to point up some of the things that apply primarily to writing for operators.

## Background

Normally you must assume that the operator brings no necessary background to reading an operator's manual. You must furnish the background. Considering that the operator is essentially a layman, the background must be kept simple. Use analogy and define all or most technical terms. Avoid mathematics altogether. Normally, avoid sending the operator to other manuals for additional information. The operator's manual should be self-contained.

Some operator's manuals are mere lists of instructions containing no background at all. In these cases the writer considers background unessential to the performance of the job. In other cases, perhaps where the typical operator represents a higher educational level or the task is more than usually complex, a good deal of background is provided.

---

[1]*Atomic Energy in Use*. Washington, D.C.: United States Atomic Energy Commission, 1967, p. 11.

[2]*Ibid*, pp. 11-12.

[3]James W. Souther, "What Management Wants in the Technical Report," *Journal of Education*, 52(8), 498-503 (1962).

[4]*Ibid*.

[5]Rudolf Flesch, *The Art of Plain Talk*, New York: Harper and Brothers, 1946, p. 38.

[6]Porter G. Perrin and George H. Smith, *Handbook of Current English*. New York: Scott, Foresman and Company, 1955, p. 211.

**Pearsall Comprehension Questions**

1. When a person moves beyond writing in school, what must be taken into consideration?

2. Name four of the five categories of audience Pearsall identifies:

3. For the layman it is necessary to provide: (Name two)

4. The executive has a concern beyond the layman's. What is it?

5. According to Pearsall, merely giving the facts to an executive is not sufficient. What else must you be prepared to present?

6. The expert seldom looks for what when reading?

## A FINAL WORD

You may consider this last test as an ending point in these reading lessons. Or, this last score may be the beginning of a lifetime of more gratifying reading in your world of work. The possibility of change lies within you and what you want.

In an effort to insure that you will continue to improve your reading abilities, you may find the following hints and drills useful.

### Chapter 7 Practice Session for the Future

HINT A. If you completed 25 percent or less of the practice exercises, you should complete the following drill on a somewhat regular basis. (3-5 times per week)

*DRILL:*

(1) Practice read for 5 minutes, using your Basic Step. Compute your speed, and mark your stopping point.
(2) Practice Read the same section in three minutes or less, using the "S." Start your recall.
(3) Read the section at a rate of from 500–750 wpm, and complete your recall. Repeat this drill in one hour sessions until you feel comfortable at 750 wpm.

HINT B. If you completed 50-75 percent of the practice exercises, you should complete the following drill in one hour sessions, 2-3 times per week.

*DRILL:*

(1) Preview a 5,000 word section in two minutes or less; begin a VDI.
(2) Read the same section in five minutes or less, and continue your recall. Repeat this drill in one hour sessions until you feel very comfortable at 1,000 wpm.

HINT C. If you completed 75 percent or more of the work, you should merely pace yourself through various types of materials at the rate of 1,000 wpm plus. In order to increase your reading speed, all that should be necessary for you to improve is that you increase your pace at the rate of 250 wpm for about five hours worth of reading time. Once you attain a rate of about 1500 wpm with some comfort, you should attempt to read the material using the "S" method. It will probably initially seem as though you're starting anew, but remember how far you've come already.
HINT D. Read everything with a purpose in mind. Determine, before you start reading, how much you want or need out of the material, as well as a rate at which you want to read it.
HINT E. Read everything using your hand. You may find that you may be able to maintain your present rate without the use of your hand, but that maintenance will be short-lived. You will soon begin to regress to your earliest reading rates.
HINT F. Finally, cementing any physical skill requires time and use of the skill. If you plan to maintain your rates, or perhaps progress even further, it is essential that you use your new skills in one way or another (at work or for pleasure reading), on a regular basis.

Learning to read efficiently is an empowering skill. Reading well connects a professional in dynamic and subtle ways to the incredibly complex and elegantly simple network of work that is your job. Become as good as you want in your field by reading well.

## Answers: Pearsall Article

1. the audience and what background it has. Why do they want to read your writing?
2. simple, interesting, practical, somewhat dramatic.
3. He must make decisions beyond and with what he reads.
4. interpretations and implications.
5. background information.

# APPENDIX

**APPENDIX A. How to Compute Words per Minute**

TO COMPUTE RATE:

WPM = Words per minute
WPP = Words per page
N = Number of pages
T = Time of reading

To determine *number of words per page (WPP):*

Cound the words in 5 full lines and divide by 5. This gives the average words per line. Then count the number of lines on a full page, including short lines, and multiply by the average words per line. This determines the words per page.

To determine Reading Rate (Words per Minute):

The words per minute (rate) is found by multiplying the words per page by the number of pages, and then dividing by the time spent.

$$\text{WPM.} = \frac{\text{WPP} \times \text{N}}{\text{No. of Min. (T)}}$$

Example: If your book has 250 WPP and you have read 10 pages in 2 minutes, then you have read 1,250 WPM.

$$125 \text{ (WPM)} = \frac{250 \text{ (WPP)} \times 10 \text{ (N)}}{\text{WPP}}$$

To find the number of pages you must read in a specified time to reach your goal, multiply the WPM by the time, then divide by the number of words on each page.

$$\text{N.} = \frac{\text{WPM} \times \text{T}}{\text{WPP}}$$

*Example:* If you want to read 1,000 WPM in 5 minutes, you will multiply 1,000 by 5, which equals 5,000. You will then divide by 250 WPP, and the answer is 20. So, you must read 20 pages in 5 minutes to accomplish your goal.

$$20 = \frac{1,000 \text{ WPM} \times 5}{250}$$

## APPENDIX B. Course Progress Chart

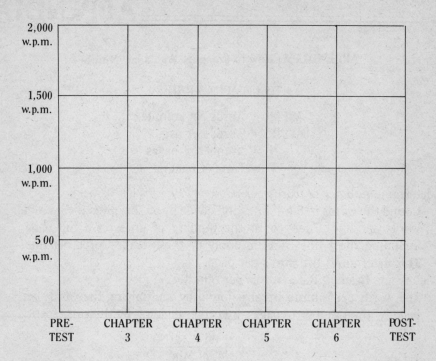

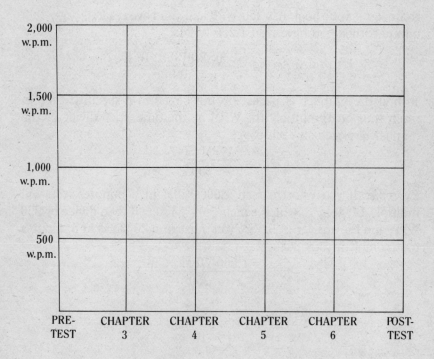

# Index